IMAGES OF
RISING SUN AT WAR

THE JAPANESE ARMY
1931-1945

RARE PHOTOGRAPHS FROM WARTIME ARCHIVES

Philip S. Jowett

Pen & Sword
MILITARY

First published in Great Britain in 2017 by
PEN & SWORD MILITARY
An imprint of
Pen & Sword Books Ltd
47 Church Street
Barnsley
South Yorkshire
S70 2AS

ISBN 978-1-47387-488-6

Typeset by Concept, Huddersfield, West Yorkshire HD4 5JL.
Printed and bound in England by CPI Group (UK) Ltd, Croydon CR0 4YY

Pen & Sword Books Ltd incorporates the imprints of Pen & Sword Archaeology, Atlas, Aviation, Battleground, Discovery, Family History, History, Maritime, Military, Naval, Politics, Railways, Select, Social History, Transport, True Crime, and Claymore Press, Frontline Books, Leo Cooper, Praetorian Press, Remember When, Seaforth Publishing and Wharncliffe.

For a complete list of Pen & Sword titles please contact
PEN & SWORD BOOKS LIMITED
47 Church Street, Barnsley, South Yorkshire S70 2AS, England
E-mail: enquiries@pen-and-sword.co.uk
Website: www.pen-and-sword.co.uk

Contents

A Japanese army mountain gun is fired by its crew during fighting in the hills of Southern China in 1938. The Japanese faced resistance in the Southern Chinese provinces from both regular and irregular Nationalist forces loyal to Chiang Kai-shek. During their campaigns in China, Japanese troops often faced difficult terrain like this.

Introduction

By the beginning of the twentieth century Japan had recently emerged from centuries of isolation from the rest of the world. It had spent the second half of the nineteenth century modernizing certain aspects of its society although still maintained many of its traditions.

The Japanese army and navy had modernized at a steady rate from the 1870s and had begun to look beyond their own shores for military adventures. In 1894 Japan went to war with the Chinese empire (Sino-Japanese War, 1894–95) which had been the dominant power in East Asia and defeated it decisively. Even though some of the gains that Japan had made from the Chinese had to be handed back to them as a result of international pressure they continued to maintain their territorial ambitions on the Asian mainland. In 1900 Japanese troops were decisive in quelling the anti-foreigner Boxer Rebellion alongside smaller military contingents from European powers and the USA. China's price for peace with the foreign powers was the granting of territorial and trading concessions to all the powers apart from the USA. These concessions gave the Japanese a foothold in China and allowed for the stationing of their troops in the region. The acquisition of Manchuria, the northern most region of China, fulfilled Japan's desire for more 'living space' for its expanding population and for natural resources for its industry. With China effectively neutralized, the only military power in Asia that could challenge the Japanese was the Russian empire. War with Russia was inevitable and in 1904 it broke out and again the Japanese were largely victorious on land and at sea (Russo-Japanese War, 1904–5). Having defeated their main regional rival Russia, Japan now faced little opposition to its planned expansion of the Asian mainland.

When the First World War broke out in August 1914 the Japanese army and navy had a new role to play as an ally of France, Great Britain and its old adversary Russia. Its first act was to capture the fortress of Tsingtao built by the Germans in their concession in Shantung province, China. The Japanese navy also took the Pacific Islands, which had formed part of the German empire before 1914. Several of these islands were to be retained by the Japanese when the German territories were being shared out after their defeat in 1918. When civil war broke out in Russian in 1918 the Japanese acted again sending a large expeditionary force into Siberia, which bordered its Manchurian concessions. Even though there were troops in the region from many European states supporting the anti-revolutionary Russian forces the Japanese remained for several years after the others had gone home, staying until 1922.

Throughout this period there was constant political conflict as Japan's civilian politicians tried to rein in the 'over ambitious' military. The civilian government did manage to secure the withdrawal of Japanese forces from Siberia and the Chinese province of Shantung. At the same time, the Imperial Army was reduced in number by four divisions in the face of fervent opposition from the military leadership.

In the mid- to late 1920s the Japanese maintained their garrisons in Manchuria and on several occasions intervened in the civil war raging throughout China. These interventions were justified on the basis that they were protecting Japanese civilians living in cities affected by the Chinese conflict. In 1928 the victory of the Chinese National Revolutionary Army (NRA) of Chiang Kai-shek threatened to unite the country for the first time in almost twenty years. The Japanese Kwangtung Army, which had been stationed in Manchuria since 1900, was determined that the unification of China under one government should not interfere with its control of parts of the province. When the Manchurian leader, Chang Hsueh-liang, agreed to join Chiang Kai-shek's government it was only a matter of time before the Kwangtung Army acted. In September 1931 plotters within the Kwangtung Army planted a bomb on the Manchurian railway. This bomb was blamed on the Chinese which gave the Japanese an excuse to attack the Nationalist garrison at Mukden. Within days the Japanese were advancing through Southern Manchuria and the Imperial Army had begun its war on China.

Acknowledgements

My thanks go as always to anyone who has assisted me over the years with information, encouragement and photographs for my publications.

The photographs used in this book are from the Philip Jowett collection unless otherwise indicated.

A group of Samurai warriors pose for the camera in a Tokyo studio in the late 1800s as a centuries old era of military tradition comes to an end. Although many of these fighters would have to adapt to the new modern ways of warfare, most retained much of their old mentality. In the wars of the early 1900s survivors from this period of Japanese military history maintained the Bushido way of life. As the century unfolded some of the humane elements of the Bushido Code, such as good treatment of prisoners, were forgotten. These were replaced with a brutal attitude which called for the military objective to be achieved no matter the cost to enemy soldier or civilian alike.

These Japanese infantrymen rest in their encampment in the hills of Manchuria during the Russo-Japanese War of 1904–5. Japan's victory in the war with Imperial Russia established them as the foremost military power in the Far East. The soldiers are wearing the new khaki summer uniform of the Imperial Army ten years before the outbreak of the First World War. Lessons from the trench warfare and heavy bombardments of the Russo-Japanese War were not really learned by the Great Powers when they went to war in August 1914.

This soldier was a member of the Japanese interventionist forces that fought in Siberia from 1918–22. In the aftermath of the Russian Revolution Japanese forces were sent to the Soviet Far East to support White Russian armies. The Japanese were virulently anti-Communist and gave short shrift to any Bolshevik prisoners they took. He is well kitted out for winter fighting with fur-lined coat, hat and gloves, and is armed with an Arisaka rifle.

This Type 11 light machine-gun team are taking part in a military manoeuvre in 1924. This photograph shows an early attempt at camouflage as the team have added foliage to their caps. One of the crew carries a cloth net to catch the spent cartridges as they are thrown out of the machine gun. At this time the Japanese were beginning to provide significant support for some of the Northern Chinese warlords fighting for control of China. Their sponsorship of the conservative Manchurian warlord Chang Tso-lin was part of their plans to gain a stronger foothold in the region.

Japanese troops are transported from their barracks to their positions while operating in the Chinese province of Shantung in the late 1920s. Japan had taken control of the German concessions in the province during the early days of the First World War. In 1928 the NRA of China was advancing into the province in pursuit of their Northern warlord enemies. In response the Japanese sent in 5,000 reinforcements to stop the NRA from taking over the city of Tsinan. The armed clashes between the Japanese and the NRA were the first of many that were to occur over the next few years.

(**Above**) Japanese troops assemble at Tientsin station in Northern China in May 1927 during their attempts to interfere in the civil conflict going on in China. The long-running war between Chiang Kai-shek's NRA and the Northern warlords under the overall command of Chang Tso-lin was coming to a head. On 30 May 2,200 Japanese troops landed in Shantung province in an attempt to stop Chiang's march on Peking. Both Chinese leaders complained about the Japanese interference in China's affairs which was to increase over the next few years.

(**Opposite, above**) Whippet medium tanks of the Japanese Imperial Army's infantry armoured force take part in manoeuvres in the mid-1920s. The Japanese purchased a handful of these British First World War armoured vehicles along with a few Mk V tanks. These were used to form two tank companies and to equip the experimental tank unit attached to the Chiba Infantry School. This school helped develop Japanese tank tactics throughout the 1920s which were to be put into action in the early 1930s. Whippets were not used in battle and were said to have been withdrawn from service in 1929.

(**Opposite, below**) A Model 4 150mm howitzer is fired from underneath a camouflage net during a 1920s' military manoeuvre. The Model 4, which came into Japanese service in 1915, was to serve until 1945 and beyond. Designed at the Osaka Arsenal, it was to remain the standard heavy howitzer until 1936 when a new model was introduced. Although its replacement, the Type 96, was produced in some numbers, the Model 4 was used in China and the Pacific Theatre.

In a typical propaganda photograph of the 1930s a line of bicycle-riding schoolboys carry rifles to show they are ready to serve the empire. As with the totalitarian regimes in Italy and Germany, images like this were meant to show that the whole Japanese nation was in military mode. Most of these school-boys would go on to serve in the Imperial Army, Navy and Air Forces during the Second World War.

(**Opposite, above**) Naval Landing Troops of the Imperial Navy pose at the side of their unit's Crossley armoured car in the late 1920s. During the various incidents that took place in the late 1920s and early 1930s it was often landing parties like this that fought the Chinese. In many cases these navy infantry would secure a town or city and hold it until the army could reinforce them. In reality the landing parties were given at best basic military training which was inadequate for their role. In 1929 the Japanese navy organized specially trained Naval Landing Forces, which were to act as the spearhead force for amphibious landings. These were to become an important element in the occupation of the Pacific Islands in 1941–2 and then in their defence in 1943–5.

(**Opposite, below**) As part of the overt militarization of Japanese society these school girls are taking part in a route march in their uniforms. The popularity of the Japanese armed forces amongst the population in the 1920s and 1930s meant that schoolchildren were usually happy to take part in military activities. Japan's military adventures on the Asian mainland were also popular with the people and the progress of them was followed avidly by most of the population.

Emperor Hirohito takes the salute at a Japanese army parade in the early years of his rule, which began in late 1926. The new emperor had dismissed his moderate Prime Minister Tanaka over the assassination of the Manchurian warlord Chang Tso-lin. Tanaka and his allies had tried in vain to control the more troublesome and maverick elements in the Kwangtung Army command. Without Tanaka's influence, the Kwangtung Army now knew that its plans for the invasion of Manchuria would meet with little opposition from Japan's emasculated politicians.

General Hideki Tojo dominated Japanese politics in the late 1930s and throughout the Second World War. He became Japanese Minister of War in 1940 and Prime Minister in October 1941 and was virtual dictator during the war. In February 1944 he became Chief of the Japanese General Staff but was forced to resign after the fall of Saipan on 22 July the same year. Tojo fully accepted that his death penalty, carried out in 1948, was the price he had to pay for his role in the war.

Chapter One

Manchuria
(1931-2)

In the late 1920s and early 1930s the Japanese presence in China was confined to the Kwangtung Army, which had the right to garrison the Japanese-owned South Manchuria Railway. Japanese military plotters within the Kwangtung Army had long-held ambitions to conquer the Chinese provinces that made up Manchuria and wrest it from Chinese government control.

During the 1910s and 1920s' Warlord period of conflict in China Manchuria had been controlled by a military strongman, Chang Tso-lin. Chang had been supported by the Kwangtung Army with arms, money and military advisors and was expected to show loyalty to his sponsors. Chang's defeat by the 'revolutionary' forces of the new Chinese leader Chiang Kai-shek in 1928 made the Japanese lose faith in him. As Chang Tso-lin withdrew into his Manchurian stronghold in 1928 his train was blown up by Japanese agents. The Kwangtung Army hoped that the assassination of their leader would force Chang's troops to attack the Japanese. This would then give the Kwangtung Army an excuse to intervene militarily in Manchuria and gain re-enforcements from Japan for the heavily outnumbered Imperial Army. They did not expect any resistance from Chang's opium addict son, Chang Hsueh-liang, 'The Young Marshal', who had inherited the leadership of the Manchurian armies. Chang Hsueh-liang and his father had been fighting Chiang Kai-shek's NRA for several years. It was expected that the Manchurian Army would continue their war against the Nationalists and the NRA. In a complete 'about face', Chang Hsueh-liang, having sought treatment for his addiction in Europe, had decided to join the NRA in late 1928 and unite his 300,000-strong military forces with Chiang Kai-shek. This loss of control of Manchuria could not be tolerated by the Japanese and the removal of the Young Marshal became a priority. By December 1930 the 30,000-strong Kwangtung Army had already set in place plans for the occupation of Manchuria. The main purpose for the planned invasion was to create a buffer zone between the Soviet Union and Northern China. Japanese paranoia about the possible spread of Communism from the Soviet Union meant that it was essential to create a bulwark in the region.

The takeover of Manchuria began on 18 September 1931 when a bomb exploded on the Japanese-owned South Manchuria Railway near the city of Mukden. The city was the headquarters of the Young Marshal and his reduced 160,000–200,000-strong army had its major arms depots there. This explosion was set off by Japanese soldiers who would use this incident as a pretext to start hostilities with the Chinese garrison. It was blamed on 'Chinese terrorists' and attacks were immediately launched against the Chinese garrisons in the city. Chang's troops in Mukden gave up without much of a fight and the city was easily taken in a few hours.

After consolidating their control of Mukden the Japanese began to advance along the railway taking towns and garrisons as they went. Within a few days all of the Kwangtung Army's strategic objectives in South and Central Manchuria had been taken. On 19 September the strategic city of Changchun fell to the Japanese and a few days later all the major cities in Manchuria were under their control. Only the North-Western city of Tsitsihar and the Southern city of Chinchow remained in Chinese hands with military forces capable of resisting the Kwangtung Army. As the Chinese troops prepared to resist any further Japanese advances they received orders from the government in Nanking which changed this. Chiang Kai-shek was convinced that the League of Nations would force the Japanese to withdraw from Manchuria and wanted them to be seen as the aggressor. He ordered the Young Marshal and his troops to retreat in front of the Imperial Army and avoid clashes at all costs. Against their wishes the Young Marshal's remaining troops withdrew south-wards beyond the Great Wall, which formed the border between Manchuria and the rest of China.

In order to make their takeover of Manchuria 'official' the Kwangtung Army, without support from the Tokyo government, decided to create a new pro-Japanese state there. In a bid to add some legitimacy to the new state they attempted to persuade the former emperor of China, Pu-Yi, to become its chief executive. It was intended that within a short period Pu-Yi could be enthroned as puppet emperor of Manchuria. On 1 March 1932 the Japanese formerly announced the creation of a new Manchurian state or 'Manchukuo'. In response to the conquest of Manchuria the Chinese population reacted by imposing a series of trade boycotts, which severely affected their industry. Japan's response to these crippling boycotts was to lead to further clashes, this time in the Chinese city of Shanghai.

Imperial Army troops march through the gates of the city of Mukden after its occupation by the Kwangtung Army. The Kwangtung Army officially had a strength of 10,000 men but in reality it had been reinforced clandestinely over a few years to nearer 20,000. On paper the Japanese were heavily outnumbered by the 250,000 or so Chinese Nationalist armies in Manchuria under the command of the Young Marshal, Chang Hsueh-liang.

(**Above**) A Japanese medium artillery battery fires towards retreating Chinese Nationalist troops in the winter of 1931–2. The guns are Model 38 75mm field guns which had been introduced into Imperial Army service in 1905. Most of the Model 38s were sent back to the Osaka Arsenal for extensive modifications during the First World War. This 'improved' Model 38 was kept in service with the Imperial Army into the early years of the Second World War.

(**Opposite, above**) Imperial Army troops march across the plains of Manchuria during their advance into the heart of the vast region previously controlled by the Young Marshal, Chang Hsueh-liang. Chang had decided to join the ranks of the Nationalist Chinese in 1929–30 having expressed his total opposition to the Japanese. His defiance was one of the triggers that decided the Japanese Kwangtung Army to strike against his North-Eastern Army. The soldiers are wearing the 2nd pattern of steel helmet introduced into service in 1930 and worn by many troops in 1931–2.

(**Opposite, below**) Two Imperial Army troops stand guard over a Sumida M2953 armoured car which has been fitted with its rail wheels so that it can run along the Manchurian railway. Entering service in 1928, the Sumida was a useful vehicle which could quickly be converted back to run on roads when necessary. When the Sumida was needed for road use the solid rubber tyres carried on the side of its hull were refitted by using internal jacks to raise it. The car was armed with a single machine gun in its rotating turret but carried a six-man crew who fired their rifles from the firing points.

A cavalry officer climbs on the metal framework of a recently captured building in the Manchurian town of Kaopangtze in February 1932 to fly the Japanese battle flag. This action shows the rest of his unit that the town and its vital railway line has been taken by his unit. Although many Chinese troops withdrew in front of the advancing Imperial Army, isolated Nationalist garrisons did choose to fight.

The crew of a Type 87 Crossley armoured car are ready to respond to any trouble as they guard the gate of a Manchurian town. This armoured car, which was based on an Indian 1925 pattern, has been modified by the Japanese and has pneumatic tyres fitted. Introduced into Japanese service in 1927, this type of car was used in large numbers by them in the early 1930s.

This machine-gunner pictured in Manchuria in the summer of 1932 is armed with a Type 11 light machine gun. He is wearing the Cherry Blossom model steel helmet with the Imperial five-pointed star embossed on the front. In this close-up the details of the machine gun are clear with its hopper for bullets on the left-hand side and a carrying strap. Underneath the machine gun the gunner has an ammunition box which has five round clips which are fed into the hopper six at a time. As the hopper needed an oil reservoir to feed the clips it was prone to jamming the breech with dirt and grit. Like other Japanese small arms, the Type 11 was both underpowered and its mechanism was over complicated.

(**Above**) A lone Japanese sentry stands guard outside the gates of his barracks which are protected by electrified barbed wire fences. Even though the Imperial Army was soon in control of Manchuria the threat of attack by the Chinese resistance was to continue into the mid-1930s. The private is wearing the M90 uniform with the Cherry Blossom model helmet and a pair of woollen gloves, probably sent in a care parcel from his family back in Japan.

(**Opposite, above**) An armoured train of the Imperial Army sits in a station before going out on patrol during the fighting in Manchuria. The visible part of the train is made up of two machine-gun wagons with rotating turrets, a sandbagged flat-bed truck and in the centre the armoured plated engine. Both machine-gun wagons have numerous firing points for crew to fire rifles from and even the engine has a couple at each side.

(**Opposite, below**) When the Japanese invaded Manchuria they seized a number of ex-Chinese armoured trains which they used in the campaign. This train has an artillery wagon at the front with a 75mm gun mounted in its rotating turret. The firing points along the side have sliding doors to stop bullets entering the wagon when they are not in use. On top of the wagon, which is camouflaged in typical Japanese pattern, stand its commanding officers.

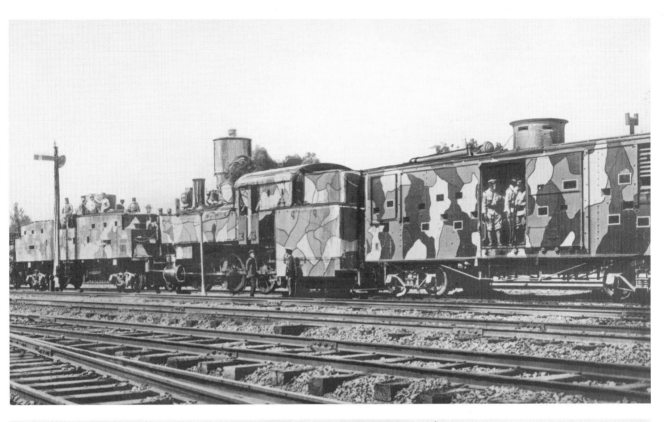

(**Above**) A rail gun mounted on the back of a specially converted flat truck opens fire on a group of Nationalist irregulars in the winter of 1931–2. The war in Manchuria was largely fought along the region's railways and the Japanese used as many armoured trains as they could in the war. As well as using captured trains from the Chinese North-Eastern Army the Kwangtung Army later developed more purpose-built ones during the early 1930s.

(**Opposite, above**) This armoured rail truck moves slowly along the railway line while its crew look for signs of Nationalist irregulars during the ongoing guerrilla war in Manchuria in 1932. One of its crew members peers out of the truck's hatch with his finger on the trigger of his captured Chinese ZB-26 machine gun. On the rails behind it is the main train with a sandbagged flat car armed with machine guns ahead of the engine.

(**Opposite, below**) A column of Japanese armoured cars and trucks drive out of their barracks in the centre of a Manchurian town in the early days of the Japanese occupation. Such demonstrations of force were often enough to keep the population in check, although the people were split between pro- and anti-Japanese elements. The two Crossley Type 87 armoured cars are armed with Vickers heavy machine guns, each manned by one of its three-man crew. The crews are obviously not expecting hostility from the population as the machine-gunners are riding on the outside. Behind the Crossleys are DAT 61 trucks, which had entered Japanese service in the late 1920s.

This 2-ton Imperial Army DAT 61 truck drives along a Manchurian city road with its crew wearing motor goggles, which suggests they may be special motorized troops. All the men are wearing the old pattern peaked cap with their M90 woollen uniforms and fly the Japanese flag from their truck. A high military presence was essential to stifle any signs of resistance by the population of Manchurian cities. This was especially the case while Chinese guerrilla resistance continued in the countryside.

The crew of a Type 11 70mm mortar prepare to fire their weapon towards Chinese positions in the spring of 1932. This weapon, which was really a high-angle infantry gun, was a little too heavy to be portable. Although not ideal in the early 1930s, it was the only mortar that the Japanese had in service until lighter versions could be developed. While the crew are still sporting their fur-lined winter hats, the weather is warm enough for them to wear their M90 woollen uniforms without outer clothing.

The six-man crew of a Type 3 medium machine gun fire their weapon in defence of their barracks in 1932. Their position is reported in the caption to be at the side of one of the railways that were vital to the fighting in 1931–3. All the crewmen are wearing the Cherry Blossom model steel helmet, which was one of several models used in Manchuria. The helmet had a cherry blossom-shaped pommel at the top, which gave this model its name. Most of the men have the 1930 winter woollen uniform, while the sergeant with the binoculars has a darker shaded version.

This highly stylized postcard from the early 1930s is an early attempt to gain enthusiasm for the war in Manchuria. The original is coloured and shows the courageous Japanese grenadiers attacking a Chinese trench. Its date is indicated by the wearing of the early pattern Cherry Blossom helmet by the Japanese troops featured.

爆彈を懷き鐵條網を破壞し全身一

(**Opposite, above**) Anti-guerrilla troops capture a suspected Chinese guerrilla during a sweep through a crop of kaoliang in the early 1930s. Any civilian captured under suspicious circumstances would have been given little chance to prove their innocence. The Japanese suspected the motives of anyone who they caught in the 'wrong place at the wrong time' and swiftly executed them after interrogation, usually without trial. On close inspection two of the Japanese soldiers are wearing body armour, which was rarely worn but would have been useful in this close-quarter fighting.

(**Opposite, below**) A Japanese infantry unit pauses during an advance as they come under fire from Chinese troops during the Manchurian Campaign of 1931–2. The standard bearer holds a unit flag that has been damaged in an earlier battle but is carried into action with pride by the soldiers. Several of the men are carrying wire reels on their backs which are used to establish radio contact between the forward units and artillery of the regiment. As they advance the wireman lets out up to 1,600ft of wire which can be rewound again as the forward and support units move up. There were a variety of types of wire and cable used by these units depending on the type of communication equipment the unit had.

(**Opposite, above**) This squad of well-equipped troops pose for the cameras with a Chinese Nationalist flag captured from guerrillas in 1932. Guerrillas fighting against the Japanese may have flown the flag of the Nationalists but received little support from them. The men are wearing of M90 winter uniform, some with the double-breasted great coat while others have a fur-lined jerkin over their tunics. All have fur-lined hats with the star badge on the front and two of the soldiers are wearing helmets over the top of them.

(**Opposite, below**) A five-machine motorcycle unit of the Imperial Army pauses during an advance through Manchuria in the winter of 1931–2. The crew is kitted out for the severe Manchurian winter and the Type 3 machine-gunners have blankets over their legs in the side car. Heavily armed motorized units like this would travel ahead of their column looking for Chinese guerrillas.

(**Above**) Volunteers of the Kwangtung Army's famous Skull Regiment pose with their unit's flag in Manchuria in 1932. The unit, led by Lieutenant Ikagami (in the centre of the group wearing glasses), was first raised in the late 1920s and went on to fight during the Manchurian Campaign and its aftermath. After 1932 the unit was renowned for its anti-guerrilla fighting in which it suffered heavy casualties. According to most reports, the unit was totally destroyed in the fighting in Jehol in 1933 during which Ikagami died alongside his men. Unlike most units of the Japanese army, the Skull Regiment had its own distinct insignia made up of a white skull and crossbones which appeared on red armbands. The unit flag was white with a red disc in the centre featuring a white skull and cross bones.

Chapter Two

Japanese Aggression in China (1932–6)

After the takeover of Manchuria by the Japanese Kwangtung Army resistance to the Imperial Army by the Chinese took a number of forms. In the aftermath of the fall of Manchuria the outpouring of Chinese indignation led to a goods boycott by the population. The already weak Japanese economy was severely affected by this and saw a 90 per cent drop in trade. The bad feeling engendered by the boycott resulted in anti-Japanese demonstrations and in attacks on some Japanese citizens. A group of five Japanese monks were assaulted by indignant Chinese civilians as they walked round the city of Shanghai in January 1932, and as a consequence one of the priests died. As a result of this, 400 members of the Japanese Youth League of Shanghai sought revenge and were confronted by Chinese police who shot one of them.

The two Japanese deaths were subsequently used as a pretext for a detachment of sailors from the Imperial Fleet and armed Japanese civilians to take to the Shanghai streets. When the confused Chinese thought that these actions were an attempt to take over the city Nationalist troops moved against the Japanese. Planes from the Japanese fleet began bombarding Chinese positions within the city, which were defended by the 22,500-strong 19th Route Army. This unit was one of the best in the Nationalist army but was independently minded and had proved itself in recent fighting against the Communists. The fighting soon escalated as the Chinese troops were determined to defend their city and the Japanese moved in reinforcements and 7,000 troops and 40 aircraft to support them. The Chinese fought well but were hampered by the fact that they did not have the air support that the Japanese had. Artillery was moved into Shanghai by both sides and resulted in heavy damage and up to 20,000 civilians casualties in the crowded streets of the city which formed the battlefield. By late February Japanese forces had been raised to a total of 50,000 Marines and soldiers and faced the 19th Route Army reinforced by the Nationalist 5th Army. Frustrated by the stubborn Chinese resistance, the Japanese increased their troops to 90,000–100,000 men and these began to outflank the Nationalist defenders. The unexpected performance of the 19th Route Army was largely against the wishes of Chiang Kai-shek, who wanted a negotiated settlement with the Japanese. When the Chinese forces were ordered to withdraw from the city a peace agreement was signed in May 1932. This agreement called for the de-militarization of Shanghai and its environs and although hard won gave the Japanese more incentives to increase pressure on the Chinese.

The leaders of the Kwangtung Army stationed in the new state of Manchukuo were not satisfied with the territory under their control. They were looking to exploit their position and expand into other provinces of Northern China. Kwangtung Army planners wanted to take over the sparsely populated province of Jehol to the north-west of Manchukuo. At the same time they wanted to establish control of regions just south of the Great Wall of China in Hopei province. In January 1933 the Japanese crossed the border between Manchukuo and Jehol and were faced by a rag-tag force of 50,000 regular and irregular Chinese troops. The Japanese were about equal in strength but had air support and a small armoured force of light tanks as well as 42,000 newly recruited Manchukuoan troops. Although the three-month campaign was successful the Imperial Army had to contend with the severe winter weather in Jehol. While Jehol was being secured Japanese troops had also advanced southwards across the Great Wall and taken up strategic positions including the coastal section of the wall at Shanhaikuan. Chinese troops defending the Great Wall were quickly defeated by the Japanese and the fighting ended with a truce. The Tangku Truce of May 1933 established a demilitarized zone in the region to the south of the Great Wall stretching down to the Peking area. The Jehol and Shanhaikuan regions were to be kept in Japanese hands with the former becoming part of the Manchukuoan empire.

In addition during the 1932–5 period, Japanese troops had to contend with a vicious guerrilla war against regular and irregular Chinese troops in Manchukuo. The Chinese who had been bypassed by the Kwangtung Army in their advance through Manchuria now formed into large guerrilla armies. These armies were made up of 300,000 ex-Nationalist soldiers and 'patriotic' bandits united only in their hatred of the Japanese. By 1933 the Japanese had 95,000 troops stationed in Manchukuo who were supported by 'unreliable' puppet troops of the Manchukuoan Army. By the mid-1930s most of the guerrillas had either been defeated in battle or had withdrawn from Manchukuo having receiving little support from the Nationalist government.

By the mid-1930s the Japanese Imperial Army had been involved in a number of campaigns in China. The army had grown to a front-line strength of 250,000 by 1936 and was a well-trained, battle-hardened force which was armed with serviceable if slightly outdated weaponry. One weakness of the Imperial Army that had affected it throughout the 1920s and 1930s was a deep division amongst its officer class. Although all officers were loyal to their emperor, they disagreed about the direction that the army should take in its military schemes in China. Many ranking officers, especially in the Kwangtung Army, would not accept any interference from civilian governments. Some Japanese officers thought that the emperor with the army behind him should be allowed to rule without recourse to any civilian politicians. Assassinations of politicians who tried to rein in the army's activities were a regular occurrence. In February 1936 one group of ultra-Nationalist army officers brought matters to a head with an attempted *coup d'état* in Tokyo. Their bid to intensify the pace of military action in China failed but the outbreak of a full-scale war with the Nationalist government was only a matter of time.

Sailors from the Imperial Navy charge through the suburbs of Shanghai during fighting with the Nationalist 19th Route Army in 1932. In their way are the bodies of several Chinese civilians killed in the crossfire in the street fighting between the two adversaries. The training of these Naval Landing Parties from the Japanese fleet moored off the coast near Shanghai left a lot to be desired. When faced by the resolute troops of the 19th Army the Japanese naval commanders had to admit that they needed assistance from their army comrades to defeat them.

Japanese Marine officers observe Chinese movements during the early stages of the fighting in Shanghai in late January 1932. One officer shouts instructions to his men before they go into action while another looks through his binoculars. As casualties amongst the Marines grew it was necessary to bring more naval infantry and soldiers into the battle. Most of the fighting for Shanghai took place in the narrow streets of the city and amongst the creeks and inlets of the Wangpoo River.

Japanese Marines sit in a gun position against the skyline of Shanghai as they wait for fighting to resume against the Chinese Nationalist garrison of the city. The gun is a Model 10 75mm naval gun which was used as an anti-aircraft or coastal defence weapon. Introduced into navy service in 1921, the Model 10 was used to defend many Pacific islands after 1941. This crew have covered the gun with camouflage netting to disguise it from a possible Chinese air attack.

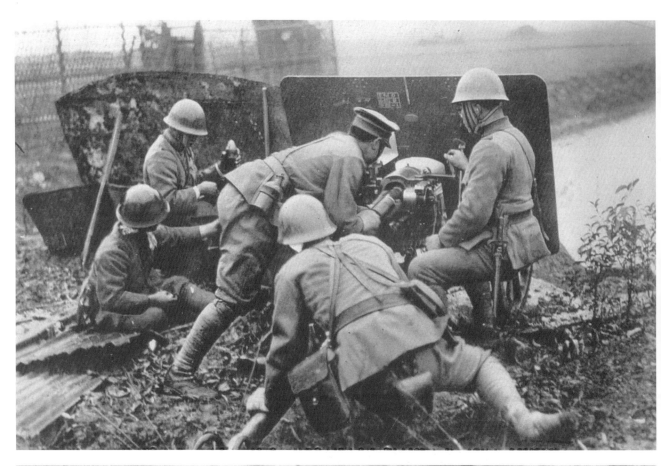

Three Japanese Marines fire towards Chinese defenders of Shanghai from behind a sandbagged position. In the initial fighting a small number of Marines and armed Japanese residents of the city were expected to deal with the Chinese garrison. They were supported by aircraft from a Japanese aircraft carrier which arrived in late January. The Chinese accused the Japanese of allowing aircraft to bomb indiscriminately in civilian areas and as a result the fighting became progressively fiercer.

(**Opposite, above**) The army crew of a light artillery piece fire towards Chinese positions on the outskirts of Shanghai in 1932. While the loader puts a shell into the gun's breech, his fellow crewmen prime more shells for him. Low-level fighting between the Japanese Marines stationed in and around Shanghai soon escalated into an artillery duel. When the Chinese 19th Army began to get the upper hand a large number of Japanese troops were landed in the city.

(**Opposite, below**) This British-made Cardon-Lloyd tankette belonging to the Imperial Navy in Shanghai is one of a handful purchased by the Japanese in the 1920s. As with several other armies in the early 1930s, the Japanese used this vehicle's design as the basis for their own light tankette, the Type 94. The lightly armed and armoured Type 94 was one of the most numerous types of armoured vehicles in service with the Japanese during the Sino-Japanese War.

(**Above, left**) Soldiers of the newly raised Manchukuoan Army are ready to advance into the Chinese province of Jehol alongside Japanese Imperial troops. The role of the puppet troops of the Japanese-created state of Manchukuo in the fighting in 1933 was mainly for propaganda purposes. Officially Jehol was claimed to belong to Manchukuo and the presence of its soldiers in its takeover was deemed to give this some credence. In reality the Japanese wanted to expand their conquests in Northern China and Jehol was chosen as the next victim of their territorial ambitions.

(**Above, right**) Two cavalry troopers photographed during the Jehol Campaign wearing the typical winter uniform of the Imperial Army. They have thick padded coats and hats which are lined with fur and woollen gloves which their families sent them. The standard bearer is holding his unit's tattered regimental standard with gold metal chrysanthemum finial and gold fringe. Flags damaged in previous campaigns were often carried with immense pride by their regiment into battle. Carbines used by the Japanese in 1933 included the Model 44, seen here, which was a relatively modern type introduced in 1911.

A motorized Japanese column moves along a mountain road during the campaign in Jehol province in early 1933 as the fighting began. An ultimatum was delivered to the leader of the Chinese North-Eastern Army, Marshal Chang Hsueh-liang, on 23 February. This called for the withdrawal of all Chinese troops from the province and was swiftly refused by Chang. Immediately the Japanese began to move motorized units like this forward to attack the Chinese defenders.

During the advance into Jehol province in early 1933 this column of Imperial Army troops struggle through the snow. The Japanese army's main problem during the winter campaign was not the Chinese troops facing them but the severe weather. With little heavy weaponry, the poorly led Chinese defenders were totally outgunned by the Japanese expeditionary force. It did not help that the Chinese commanding officer took the first opportunity to desert his men and leave them to their fate.

(**Opposite, above**) A Type 89-KO medium tank advances through a Chinese town during the fighting for the province of Jehol. Based on the British Vickers Mark C tank, the Type 89 was in 1933 a modern and potent tank and had no armoured opposition to deal with. The number of armoured vehicles used by the Japanese in Jehol was small but they performed a vital role during the campaign.

(**Opposite, below**) A French-built FT-17 light tank of the Japanese Imperial Army clatters through the streets of Shanhaikwan, the city where the Great Wall reached the Chinese coast, in February 1933. In 1922 the Japanese had purchased a number of these tanks and given them the designation *Ko-Gata Sensha*. All the tanks were armed with 37mm guns and were used alongside British Whippets until 1929 when these were withdrawn from service. The *Ko-Gata Senshas* were used throughout the 1930s and some were still in service until 1940 in China. All Japanese tanks in the 1930s had the five-pointed star symbol of the army stencilled on their frontisplate.

During fighting in Manchuria in the early 1930s a Imperial Army soldier is using a local camel to pull a cart. The Japanese were well known for adapting to whatever conditions they faced during the campaigns in China. In the bitter winter weather the soldier is wearing whatever winter gear he can get hold of. His padded coat has a fur collar and his winter hat is also lined with fur and his gloves could be army issue or sent by his family.

(**Opposite, above**) Tough-looking Japanese troops guard a troop train in a depot near the front during the Jehol Campaign. The soldiers are wearing a mixture of early 1930s' winter uniforms including fur-lined surcoats or jerkins and fur hats. Several of the men are wearing canvas-framed goggles which were normally used by motorized or armoured troops. Two soldiers on the right stand out from the rest and may belong to the Railway Protection Corps which was raised to protect Manchurian railways.

(**Opposite, below**) A Japanese commander watches as his troops march past him during the advance into the Northern Chinese province of Jehol as part of the campaign there in January 1933. He, like his men, is wearing a woollen balaclava underneath his field cap to combat the extreme cold of the winter. His body guards have stacked their Arisaka rifles in front of the general and he also has a unit standard in its canvas case propped against the rifles.

(**Above**) After an anti-guerrilla sweep through the Manchurian countryside in 1933 three Chinese peasants have been captured by Japanese cavalry. During their operations the Japanese considered any males who fell into their hands as guerrillas and their innocence or guilt was of little concern to them. The officer in the foreground will probably call for the local population to be gathered around so that they can see the fate of anyone who resists Japanese rule. He is armed with an 1886 cavalry officer's sword, which he may use to execute the poor prisoners.

(**Opposite, above**) This comic propaganda postcard issued by the Japanese in the early 1930s shows victorious Imperial troops celebrating a banzai, the traditional Japanese victory cheer. They are surrounded by the bodies of Chinese irregulars who they have defeated in fighting in Manchuria. These rather surreal cards were issued from the early 1930s until the close of the Pacific War and featured various aspects of military life.

(**Opposite, below**) The savagery of the fighting between the Japanese army and Chinese guerrilla fighters in Manchuria from 1931 to the mid-1930s is epitomized by this image. An anti-guerrilla unit of the Imperial Army has captured a group of fighters and has already executed a number of them, displaying their heads as trophies. Unless the Japanese are willing to allow the remaining fighters to join the puppet Manchukuoan Army they will face the same gruesome fate. Stacked at the side of the prisoners are their rifles and in front of the table is a ZB-26 machine gun from the Nationalist army.

Young officer recruits of the Imperial Army take part in physical exercise in the summer of 1936. At this time the Japanese armed forces could have their pick of the more than willing and patriotic volunteers who came forward. Officers were trained for seven-and-a-half years before they could even reach the rank of 2nd lieutenant. They attended military school for three years, junior military academy for two years and spent six months with their designated unit. After this they returned to do one year and ten months at the senior military academy before a final two-month stint with their unit. During this training period they were largely kept away from society in an attempt to create a total martial spirit.

(**Opposite, above**) Japanese troops taking part in a military coup in Tokyo march out of the house of a politician who they have assassinated. In the 1930s the Japanese Imperial Army officers were divided roughly into two factions which tried to control the army and influence the government. In February 1936, 1,500 members of the *Kadoha*, or Imperial Way Faction, launched a *coup d'état* in Tokyo. The *Kadoha* faction targeted a list of civilian politicians who they thought were holding back the Imperial ambitions of Japan. After the coup's defeat only 100 of the conspirators were court-martialled as the weak Japanese government could not face removing a large number of officers from the army.

(**Opposite, below**) Troops loyal to the civilian Japanese government control a busy street in Tokyo during the attempted military coup in February 1936. Known as the 'February 26 Incident', or the 'Young Officers' Revolt', the failed coup was intended to return Japan to true Imperial rule. The *Kadoha* faction was opposed by the *Toseiha* faction, known as the 'Control Faction', which had the same pro-Imperialistic aims as the other group. They differed only in the methods they adopted, the *Toseiha* being prepared to work within the political system. In contrast, the *Kadoha* were willing to take more drastic action as previous assassinations of politicians from the early 1930s bore witness.

Chapter Three

The Outbreak of the
Sino-Japanese War
(1937)

The outbreak of a full-scale war between Nationalist China and the Japanese empire became inevitable during the 1930s. There had been fighting between the two armies in Manchuria in 1931, Shanghai in 1932 and in Jehol and Northern China in 1933. Between 1934 and 1936 there had also been small-scale campaigns in Inner Mongolia and Northern China. When Japanese troops stationed around Peking and the Nationalists clashed in July 1937 a local incident soon escalated into all-out war. Both sides rushed reinforcements to the region and although previous outbreaks of fighting had been settled by local truces, this time was different. The Japanese sent five divisions into Northern China while the Nationalist army also rushed reinforcements to the front line. In the first few weeks the fighting was confined to Northern China where the Japanese army defeated the Nationalist troops stationed there before taking the old capital of Peking on 29 July.

At the same time units of the Imperial Army were advancing into the provinces that made up Inner Mongolia. A few months before the Japanese-supported Inner Mongolians had tried to capture Chahar and Suiyuan provinces and had been thrown back by the Chinese. This time the Japanese took the provinces and completed their domination of Northern China. Japan's original plan to separate the five provinces of Northern China from the rest of the country was now within reach. However, the relatively easy victories the Imperial Army had achieved against the Nationalist army meant they now widened their ambitions.

Beginning in early August, Shanghai, the commercial centre of China, had been the scene of an epic battle which eventually involved 500,000 Chinese and 300,000 Japanese. The battle started with clashes between 4,000 Japanese Marines and the Shanghai garrison and soon escalated into a major engagement. Within days forces of about 20,000 were involved on each side with the Nationalist determination to defend Shanghai leading to more and more troops being committed to its defence. By mid-September the Japanese forces in and around Shanghai had grown to

200,000 men in five divisions. Fighting continued into early November and Chinese casualties were estimated to be at least 130,000 dead.

When the Chinese withdrew from Shanghai on 7 November their orderly withdrawal soon turned into a chaotic retreat. The battle was a disaster for China with the Nationalist army having lost the cream of its better trained and equipped divisions. It was also costly for the Japanese whose 9,000 dead were deemed to be unacceptable losses by their commanders. As their armies prepared to advance further into Central China during November the Japanese Imperial Army in Northern China now totalled about 280,000 men.

Some of the defeated and demoralized Chinese troops from Shanghai now made up the garrison of the next Japanese target, the Nationalist capital Nanking. The city was politically important to Chiang Kai-shek and his government but he realized that it was not easy to defend. Its poorly commanded 100,000 defence force was a mix of raw recruits and defeated veterans who were badly organized in units that had been mixed up and as a result morale was very low. Some of the garrison were withdrawn before the battle began and the remainder were not in the right frame of mind to fight the Japanese. Chaos and panic overtook the Nanking garrison and its civilian population as the 50,000 Japanese advanced and anyone who could get out of the city did.

When the city fell on 13 December a massacre of captured Chinese soldiers and civilians began and lasted for six weeks. Beginning with Nationalist soldiers who were shot, drowned, burnt or buried alive, the killing soon spread to all males they captured. Women and children were also killed in large numbers and all females were liable to be raped often before being executed. Mass rapes followed the initial killings with few women surviving their ordeal and victims ranged from 10 to the old and infirm. Estimates of the number of Chinese killed and injured during the massacres are still debated but the lowest estimate was 42,000 and the highest an exaggerated 300,000. Reasons for the massacre have long been debated but one explanation is that it was an organized attempt to shock the Nationalist government into asking for peace. This is supported by reports that the Japanese soldiers did not kill in a frenzy but in a disciplined fashion under the orders of their officers. Whatever the reasons behind the killings and rapes it was not just Nanking that suffered under Japanese occupation. The Imperial Army's mistreatment of the Chinese people did not subdue the population but just convinced the Nationalists that surrender was not an option.

A light machine-gun squad protect the operator of the Type 11, covering him with their Arisaka rifles. They are fighting close to the Northern Chinese city of Tientsin in late July during the first days of the Sino-Japanese War. At this stage of the war they are carrying all before them as the Chinese Nationalist army struggles to contain the Imperial Army's advance.

(**Opposite, above**) An infantry unit shelters behind a hastily prepared sandbagged position during fighting for Langfang in Northern China in July 1937. After the initial fighting between the Imperial Army and the Nationalist 29th Army at the Marco Polo Bridge in early July the Japanese continued their advance. They moved forward through Northern China in late July and took the city of Tientsin on the 30th and the old capital of Peking on the 31st before fighting shifted to the coastal cities including Shanghai. These troops are wearing the summer version of the Imperial Army uniform and are all armed with the Arisaka Type 38 rifle.

(**Opposite, below**) Two crewmen fire their Type 92 70mm infantry gun during fighting in Northern China in the summer of 1937. Although the full crew of this artillery piece was up to ten men, once it was emplaced two or three men could operate it. Stacked in front of the gunners are metal cases that carry spare shells for the gun with three per case. The Type 92 was a lightweight weapon with a relatively short range of 2,800, compared to the 10–14,000 metres of a 75mm field gun.

A Japanese tank unit moving cautiously through the streets of a village in Shansi province during the fighting of 1937. The fact that several of the tank commanders are stood up in their turrets shows they are not expecting much resistance. Vehicles employed by the unit are a mixture of Type 89 medium tanks and Model 94 tankettes. Japanese military theorists fully appreciated the value of armour and by 1937 the Imperial Army had a great deal of experience in this kind of warfare.

(**Opposite, above**) The soldiers of an infantry unit of the Imperial Army wade across one of the rivers of Northern China during the first few months of the war. Their officers ride their horses across the river to act as a safety net in case any of their men lose their footing. In order to save their uniforms the men have stripped to their underwear and hold their rifles over their heads. Natural barriers like rivers and mountains were overcome at least in the early years of the war in China by the morale of the Japanese soldiers.

(**Opposite, below**) A civilian truck is used by the Imperial Army to transport them to the front line near to Peking. Although the troops have camouflaged the truck in case of air attack, the Chinese air force was not a significant threat during the 1937 fighting in Northern China. During the fighting for Peking the Chinese Nationalist garrison put up little fight against the Japanese. Troops like these ambushed the retreating garrison as it withdrew into the city and the Nationalist commander General Chao Teng-yu and his staff killed by an air strike.

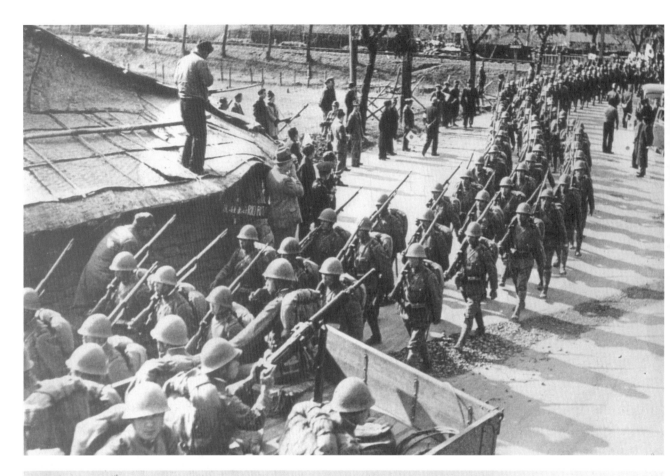

(**Opposite, above**) A long column of infantry snakes through a Chinese town that has been recently occupied by their comrades in 1937. Some townspeople are gathered to greet the soldiers as they march through with conveniently issued Japanese flags. In the truck at the head of the column a machine-gunner aims his mounted weapon towards the surrounding rooftops in case of guerrilla activity. Once a Chinese town or village had been taken the population had usually been cowed into submission and any resistance was brutally repressed.

(**Above**) The wire crew of an infantry unit moves into the outskirts of a Chinese village burdened with their equipment but ready to defend themselves if necessary. As the first man goes forward his comrade feeds the communication wire behind him to the support troops behind. In addition to their wire equipment, the men both have bundles over their shoulders to carry personal gear and leather pouches for technical kit. Hanging from the rear soldier's belt is a torch which may be military issue but appears to be a civilian item.

(**Opposite, below**) Imperial Army troops march in the torrential rain during fighting in Northern China in the autumn of 1937. The poor infantry have only their basic uniform to protect them from the elements ,while the artillerymen behind them seem to all have rain ponchos or mantles. Most of the infantrymen have entrenching tools sticking out of the back of their rucksacks and they carry their duffel bags on their left hips, which suggests they contain grenades or spare ammunition.

(**Above**) The flag unit of an Imperial Army infantry regiment marches towards the camera while the forward soldier looks confidently at the cameraman. Japanese troops appear to have spent a great deal of time marching up to their knees across Chinese rivers, streams and flooded fields. They were hardy souls who had learnt through their rigorous training and route marches that it was no use complaining and the men faced hardship with stoicism. This unit's flag has the sixteen-rayed rising sun in the centre with the usual three-sided gold cherry blossom finial. It also has a purple fringe around the field and the regimental number is featured on the white patch on the lower fly.

(**Opposite, above**) The crews of Type 94 tankettes are put through their paces with their vehicles in front of a Chinese medieval arch in 1937. The commander in the lead tank has a pair of command flags to control the unit in the field as no radios were fitted to these tanks. A company of these light tanks was allocated to each infantry division and usually used in the reconnaissance role. Type 94s were poorly armoured up to a maximum of 12mm and were just about resistant to small arms' fire.

(**Opposite, below**) A platoon of Type 94 tankettes advances across the open plains of Northern China in the first few months of the Sino-Japanese War in the autumn of 1937. These two-man light tanks were designed at a time when Italy, Great Britain, the Soviet Union and several other nations were employing similar light armoured vehicles. By 1937 these lightly armoured and armed tanks were obsolete apart from in the reconnaissance role but still continued in Japanese service until 1945.

Two Japanese soldiers man the guard post at the entrance to their camp in Northern China in 1937. The Japanese soldier was usually well equipped for the bitter winter weather faced by the Imperial Army in China. Both men are wearing the M90 greatcoat with fur collar and cuffs and also have the fur-lined winter hat. One man has an early pattern knapsack on his back with a blanket rolled on the top and attached with straps.

(**Opposite, above**) In this comic propaganda postcard from the 1930s a tank unit advances as screaming Chinese troops scatter in front of them. The racial stereotypes exhibited and the disdain shown for the Chinese enemy while intended to be comical is rather sinister. It shows the total racial superiority felt by the Japanese over their foes and which would result in the mistreatment of any Chinese soldiers captured. The bubbles coming from the Japanese tankers and Chinese infantry have captions which reinforce these stereotypes.

(**Opposite, below**) A Japanese patrol brings in a trussed up Chinese Nationalist soldier of the Northern forces resisting the Imperial Army in the autumn 1937. The Japanese have tied the soldier's shovel around his neck and have draped his rifle over his shoulders. One of the men is carrying a peaked cap taken from one of the prisoner's dead comrades as a battle souvenir. Both regular and irregular Chinese troops were usually executed by the Japanese and the fate of this man is probably already sealed.

Japanese reinforcements for the epic Battle for Shanghai in late 1937 are getting ready to disembark from their navy transports in the city. The Japanese began the battle with only 8,000 Marines of their Naval Landing Forces but were shocked by the heavy resistance of the Nationalist troops. In November forty transports full of Imperial Army 10th Army troops joined the battle at the same time as more Chinese troops were being sent to Shanghai. After ten weeks of fighting the Japanese had suffered 40,000 casualties including 9,000 dead. When the city finally fell to the Imperial Army both sides were exhausted with the Japanese moving southwards towards the Chinese capital of Nanking.

The supply column of a Japanese division moves through the snow-covered streets of a Northern Chinese town in the winter of 1937–8. Although most of the pack animals in the convoy are mules and donkeys, a lone camel carries some of the heavy equipment. Unusually the troops are wearing just their winter woollen jackets and have not put on their winter coats and hats.

The crew of a 75mm mountain gun fires towards a Chinese-held concrete bunker during fighting in Central China in 1937. Most of the crew have camouflaged themselves with netting to mould into the grasslands they are operating in. Throughout the Sino-Japanese War any inadequacies in the Imperial artillery and its guns was nullified by their numerical supremacy over the Nationalist army.

(**Above**) This cavalry trooper poses rather bizarrely with a carrier pigeon resting on the barrel of his Arisaka carbine during the winter of 1937–8. The trooper is wearing a greatcoat with high collar and winter gloves and has a canvas satchel over his shoulder. Carrier pigeons were still in widespread use in the Imperial Army alongside radio and other modern communications systems. Photographs like this were featured in the numerous pictorial magazines that kept the avid Japanese population informed about the popular war in China.

(**Opposite, above**) An artillery unit moves its gun up a steep slope in China as the rest of their unit snakes behind it in the distance. The crew's mule is straining to pull the mountain gun carriage while carrying the frame for the barrel on its back. Like other armies of the 1930s, the Imperial Army relied heavily on draught animals to transport artillery. Luckily for exposed Japanese units like this in China enemy guerrillas were not a real problem in 1937.

(**Opposite, below**) Before an attack on a Chinese town a gun crew move their Model 92 70mm howitzer into position during fighting in the autumn of 1937. The Model 92 was an effective infantry support weapon which was light in weight at only 468lb. As can be seen here, the gun could be hauled easily by a single horse or mule and could fire either high-explosive or armour piercing shells.

(**Above**) This photograph of 56-year-old Lieutenant General Kiyoshi Katsuki, the commander of the North China Garrison Army, was taken in mid-August 1937 at his headquarters in Tientsin. The general had replaced the previous commander Lieutenant General Kanichiro Tashiro, who had died a few days after the war with China broke out. When this photograph was taken the general had only a week left before he was replaced on 26 August. He was then put in command of the 1st Army in China until the end of May 1938 after which he retired from active service.

(**Opposite, above**) In a posed propaganda photograph a group of happy Chinese children salute as they try on the helmets of their new found 'friends'. Some half-hearted attempts may have been made locally to win the 'hearts and minds' of the Chinese people, but the treatment meted out to most civilians during the Sino-Japanese War makes this image somewhat sinister. Although some peasants may have been allowed to carry on their lives as before, they were always under the scrutiny of the Japanese. Any resistance by the people to Japanese rule was usually dealt with without mercy by the Imperial Army.

(**Opposite, below**) Imperial Army troops line the streets of Nanking as their commander General Matsui marches triumphantly into the city in late December 1937. Matsui was the commander-in-chief of the newly created Central China Expeditionary Force, which fought its first battle under that title at Nanking. By the time the general rode into the city the devastation caused by the battle for the city had been largely cleared away. The slaughter that took place in Nanking after its capture saw the death of many thousands of captured Chinese soldiers and civilians. It is still heavily disputed how many died in the aftermath of the fall of the city but murder, mass rape and looting were certainly tolerated by some Japanese officers and encouraged by others. Chinese figures for the slaughter at Nanking start at 200,000 while Japanese historians claim that the total killed and wounded was 42,000.

Chapter Four

The Sino-Japanese War
(1938–41)

After the first few months of the Sino-Japanese War the Nationalist army was in almost continuous retreat for the next four years. In 1938 the Japanese continued their advances through Central China and made a number of landings on the Eastern and Southern coasts. For most of the year the Japanese Imperial Army in China, now grown to a strength of twenty-four divisions, concentrated on capturing the main cities of Central China.

The tri-city of Wuhan, made up of the cities of Hankow, Wuchang and Hanyang, was the industrial centre of Nationalist China. After the fall of Nanking in December 1937 Hankow was made the new capital and both armies prepared to fight for it and its sister cities. Before Hankow could be attacked the Japanese first had to capture the strategic city of Hsuchow, which was defended by 400,000 Chinese troops. Eight Japanese divisions advanced against the city and it fell in March 1938, but this victory was followed by a rare defeat for the Imperial Army. In April an overconfident Japanese force was lured into the town of Taierhehwang and was surrounded by a large Chinese army. During the two-week battle the Japanese lost 14,000 men and should have learnt that victory against the Nationalist army could not be taken for granted. This defeat for the Imperial Army did not really impact on their campaigns in China and by May they had taken Hsuchow. More and more Japanese troops were being sucked into the battle for China and the army's strength increased from twenty-four divisions in 1938 to twenty-seven in 1940 and fifty-one divisions in 1941.

In the summer of 1938 the colossal battle for Wuhan had begun with over 380,000 Imperial troops battling the 800,000 of the Nationalist force. The tri-city fell in October and Nationalist losses were estimated at 1 million regular and irregular troops. Japanese losses in the campaign were relatively heavy and doubts had begun to be expressed as to whether the war in China could be won. During the next few years the Japanese continued to gain territory in China but the continuing resistance by the Chinese saw several large-scale counterattacks.

In 1939 the Japanese army had twenty-five divisions in China and faced a a large-scale 'Winter Offensive' by the Nationalists, which exhausted the last of the Chinese army's regular divisions. This failed Nationalist offensive was followed in the summer of 1940 by an attack by their rivals the Communists. Called the 'Hundred Regiments' offensive, this purely Communist operation was initially successful but the Imperial Army soon recovered and defeated the guerrillas. In the aftermath of both offensives the Imperial Army ran amok in the countryside punishing any civilians who they thought had supported the Nationalists and Communists. By 1941 the Imperial Army, which had grown to nearly a million men, had been fighting in China over four years, and the Japanese still controlled most of the major cities of Northern, Central and Southern China. Even though they had defeated the Nationalist Army in conventional battles again and again, the final defeat of the Chinese government eluded them.

Despite the fact that Japanese losses during the four years were much lighter than their Chinese foes these were still heavy. Between July 1937 and the end of 1940 the Imperial Army had lost 106,000 dead in action and another 30,500 wounded and 34,000 dying from disease. Losses amongst officers were particularly heavy and their replacements were not up to the standard of their predecessors. Morale amongst the

rank and file of the Imperial Army also began to suffer with defeatism becoming common amongst front-line units. One piece of graffiti written on a Chinese wall summed up this low morale, 'Fighting and death everywhere and now I am wounded. China is limitless and we are like drops of water in an ocean. There is no purpose in this war. I shall never see my home again.' The war in China was to continue for another four years and the number of troops committed to it remained high. In reality the Japanese knew that the war would not be won in China and the policy of 'holding ground' was the dominant one amongst the officers and men of the Imperial Army until 1945.

This Japanese soldier poses wearing the new Type 98 woollen winter uniform of 1938 with field cap, tunic, breeches and puttees with canvas straps wrapped around in an X pattern. He has full marching kit of leather knapsack, canvas haversack and a leather strapped water bottle on his right hip. Over his right shoulder he wears the canvas bag for his gas mask and on his belt he has two leather ammunition pouches. The rifle is a Type 99 Arisaka with folding wire monopod attached to the fore stock to steady it when firing from a prone position.

After landing on the Southern coastline of China in 1938 radio operators establish contact with neighbouring units. The transmitter used by these operators is the smallest type in service with the Imperial Army and Navy. One of the weaknesses of the Japanese army was its poor communication equipment which lagged behind that of other combatants. According to the US intelligence reports of the period, the Japanese preferred to rely on wire communications once a position had been established. These kind of transmitters and receivers would then be relegated to a secondary role within the unit. The radio man in the foreground of the picture is wearing the two-toed *tabi* shoe, which was favoured by many Japanese soldiers.

An officer and his men carry blocks of ice across a frozen river to take back to their camp to be melted for drinking water. The man at the rear is punting their sledge over the ice and has even attached a Japanese flag to his oar. This photograph was taken in January 1938 alongside the Tientsin–Pukow railway near Tsinan in Shantung province. The winter gear worn by the soldiers is incomplete, the officer wearing a fur hat, the man with the rifle a fur collar and ear muffs and their comrade just basic uniform. Shortly after this photograph was taken the city of Tsinan surrendered to the Imperial Army.

In the morning mist a heavy field gun of the Imperial Army fires towards Chinese positions. The gun is a Model 4 150mm field howitzer which had entered service with the Japanese in 1915. Although a new howitzer had been introduced in 1929, the older gun was still in widespread use throughout the war. The newer model outranged this gun by over 10,000m but the Model 4 was still superior to most guns in Chinese service in 1938.

(**Above**) The high attrition of draught animals during the war in China is well illustrated in this photograph. Crews of two medium field guns are attempting to haul their guns and limbers along a road using ropes. These 75mm guns were normally drawn by up to six horses so these men are performing a mammoth task which would only have been possible over short distances.

(**Opposite, above**) An Imperial Army infantry unit crosses a shallow river in 1938. The men have stripped down to their underwear to keep their trousers dry, draping them over their shoulders and backpacks, their boots hanging from their belts. Most of the men are armed with the standard Arisaka Model 38 rifle while the machine-gunner carries his Type 11. Units were vulnerable to attack while overcoming an obstacle like this but here the troops are being covered by their comrades on the bank out of shot.

(**Opposite, below**) During a lull in the fighting in China in 1938 these Imperial Army engineers practise erecting and positioning an infantry assault bridge. The bridge was intended to allow infantrymen to cross in single file and was designed to be easily built from its light welded steel sections. Its kapok (buoyant tree fibre) floats carried the weight of the soldiers crossing the 3ft-wide boarding that made up its surface.

(**Opposite, above**) An infantry unit takes up a defensive position along a railway track during the 1938 summer campaign in China. This photograph shows the typical make-up of an infantry platoon of the Imperial Army: 54 rifle men with 3 light machine guns and 3 grenade launchers. Unlike their Chinese adversaries, the Japanese only used a few models of machine guns and rifles as well as utilizing captured weaponry.

(**Opposite, below**) Infantry move at the double through woodland during their advance in Shansi province, North-West China in the summer of 1938. The Imperial Army had captured most of the province in late 1937 but Chinese Nationalist forces held on to a few small regions. Although the Japanese could take cities and other urban districts, controlling the vast rural areas was proving difficult. Huge numbers of troops were needed to try and subdue the Chinese resistance throughout the late 1930s and early 1940s.

(**Above**) Soldiers gather around their comrade who is demonstrating the anti-aircraft sight fitted to a Chinese machine gun they have captured. The heavy machine gun is a Czechoslovakian supplied ZB-53, which was sold to Nationalist China in large numbers in the 1930s. In most cases any captured weaponry was used by the Japanese as long as sufficient amounts of ammunition were taken with them.

(**Opposite, above**) A machine-gunner and his loader aim their Type 3 heavy machine gun, which was introduced in 1914. The Type 3 was a modified version of the French Hotchkiss and given the nickname the 'woodpecker' because of the noise it made. Interestingly one man wears his ranks on his shoulder boards in the pre-1937 style, while his comrade has his on his collar in the modern style.

(**Opposite, below**) In this chaotic scene Japanese reinforcements are landed by barges on one of the rivers of Shantung province in May 1938. This region had seen heavy fighting between the Japanese and the Chinese Nationalist army in the first few months of the year. The Japanese high command hoped that these extra troops would crush any further stubborn resistance in Shantung. As can be seen here, the Japanese soldier had to carry a lot of kit on the march to the front line when trucks or draught animals were not available.

(**Above**) Troops with bayonets fixed rush through Nanchang railway station during the battle for the city in March 1939. These men are part of 11th Corps under the command of General Neiji Okamura who continued to fight for Nanchang's control until late April. Desperate Chinese attempts to re-take the city after it had fallen in March were beaten back by the Japanese. According to reports of the battle, the Japanese used gas dropped from aircraft on several occasions during the fighting.

(**Above**) Soldiers advance across a newly constructed bridge on the outskirts of the recently occupied city of Nanchang in the spring of 1939. The bridge has been constructed by Imperial Army engineers who were experts in the building of wooden trestle bridges like this. Although this type of bridge looks fairly flimsy, it was capable of taking heavy equipment. Japanese engineers had a wide range of bridges for crossing streams and rivers, including assault ones for infantry and pontoon ones used for armour and artillery. Metal- section bridges were used by the Japanese but they seemed to have favoured the wooden type.

(**Opposite, above**) In a scene typical of any occupied city in Northern China a group of Imperial troops watch over crowds of Chinese civilians who are keeping a safe distance in 1939. Controlling the population alongside the Japanese soldiers are a number of unarmed 'puppet' policemen given the task of crowd control. When the Japanese occupied a city or town they soon established puppet authorities, the officials of which were given the task of administering the population. These collaborationist civilians often had the backing of former policemen who were willing to serve the Japanese.

(**Opposite, below**) An officer in a reconnaissance unit in China writes a despatch which will be put in the leather envelope on the collar of the messenger dog. Presumably the dogs were used to pass messages over short distances to save troops from coming under enemy fire. The Imperial Army divisional signal unit was made up of 250 men who operated the various types of communication equipment. These included telephones, ground to air radio sets, standard radio sets, helio lamps and semaphores. As well as messenger dogs like these, the signal unit also employed carrier pigeons when mechanical means of communication were unavailable.

A Japanese sentry stands guard at his post during an anti-guerrilla operation in Northern China in 1940. By this stage of the Sino-Japanese War the Imperial Army in Northern China was dealing with more and more resistance from Communist guerrillas. This soldier is well equipped for the winter campaigning with coat, hat and fur-lined gloves. He also has fur-lined padded anklets which are worn over the top of the standard army boot.

(**Opposite, above**) A group of officers and men stand chatting outside their billet in the summer of 1940. This photograph provides a good record of uniforms worn by the Imperial Army. Most soldiers are wearing the M38 tunic, while one man wears a modified M30 tunic and all have standard field caps. On the left of the picture one man has a 1938 pattern greatcoat and all uniforms are in varying shades of khaki. Several men have the weekly duty red and white armband, while the officer in the centre has the sash that denotes the same duty.

(**Opposite, below**) Japanese troops carrying heavy packs wade across a stream during an anti-guerrilla operation in China in October 1941. The unit's machine-gunner is at the front of the group with a Model 96 light machine gun without magazine fitted, so they are obviously not expecting to come under fire during the crossing. In the background a few mounted soldiers appear to be having a discussion mid-stream which again suggests they are not worried about guerrilla attacks.

A sentry on guard duty outside his unit's encampment in China in 1941. He has his bayonet fixed in readiness on his Type 38 rifle. On his head he has a mosquito headcover and he is wearing a pair of anti-mosquito gloves. The headgear may look a little ridiculous but it was an essential part of a soldier's kit when serving in a malarial region. Japanese uniforms were practical and protective items like this were issued to troops when available.

(**Opposite, above**) This anti-guerrilla operation in the summer of 1941 looks to be a pretty disorganized affair with soldiers moving forward at a leisurely pace. The performance of the Imperial Army had begun to deteriorate from 1938 once it became obvious that the Chinese were stubbornly refusing to capitulate. After four years of war in China an almost inevitable war weariness set in amongst many of the Japanese troops serving there. Continued Chinese resistance combined with the vast distances that the Imperial Army had to cover sapped the Japanese morale. High casualties, especially amongst the officer class, gradually reduced the quality of units and many soldiers stopped believing in a final victory in China. Many soldiers began to think that they would never see home again and a negative fatalism pervaded the ranks.

(**Opposite, below**) A unit of Type 94 tankettes muster for an anti-guerrilla operation in support of an infantry unit in the winter of 1940–1. The Type 94 was still an important element in the Japanese armoured forces in China in 1941 and continued in use until 1945. On the rear of the tankettes' turrets are several types of unit insignia, the vehicle in the middle distance featuring a cherry blossom. Field signs on tanks were usually made up of white painted geometric symbols, Arabic numerals and Japanese characters used in a complicated system. The crewmen are wearing a mixture of winter overalls, winter overcoats and padded winter crash helmets for the chilly weather they will face during the operation.

Well-camouflaged troops move forward cautiously during an attack against Chinese guerrillas in the summer of 1941. The men are wearing the M98 tropical shirt, breeches and puttees with foliage attached to their 1932 Model steel helmets. Most of the men are armed with Arisaka rifles, while one man is armed with a captured Chinese ZB-26 light machine gun. By 1941 the recruits arriving in China were not up to the standard of those that had started the war four years earlier. The original criteria for recruits had to be relaxed as is evidenced by the number of shortsighted troops wearing glasses by this date.

Imperial Army troops scramble up a hill during an operation in China in the summer of 1941. The soldiers are wearing summer uniforms and have attached foliage to their steel helmets; they are armed with Type 38 carbines with bayonets fixed. By 1941 the Imperial Army had over 2,000,000 under arms but the long drawn out campaign in China was beginning to put a strain on its human resources. In that year 714,000 men were examined for military service but only 330,000 were passed fit to serve.

By 1944, when this photograph was taken, the Japanese Imperial Army in China was suffering a shortage of reliable replacements and equipment. Although the Japanese did not want to reduce the number of troops in China, the standard of both men and weaponry was gradually being depleted. These young volunteers are serving in Northern China and have been sent there to act as armed farmers combining tending to crops with fighting guerrillas. Their rifles are captured Chinese Gew 88s and it appears that some of the soldiers have not been issued with any weapons.

A Japanese soldier lights the cigarette of a Chinese soldier of the Nanking Army during a joint anti-guerrilla operation in 1942. The Nanking Army was raised by the puppet government of Wang Ching-wei, which had been itself organized by the Japanese in 1940. Although there were several hundred thousand of these puppet troops operating against the Communist guerrillas, they were largely ineffective. This propaganda image belies the fact that the Japanese soldier had little respect for his Chinese 'allies'.

Chapter Five

'Nomonhan' – Japan's War with the Soviet Union (1938–9)

While the Japanese Imperial Army fought its campaigns in China from 1931 they also kept an eye on their possible rivals for power in the Soviet Union. Since the Japanese-controlled puppet state of Manchukuo had a common border with both Soviet Siberia and the pro-Soviet Mongolian People's Republic (MPR) armed clashes were almost inevitable. In the mid-1930s several small-scale skirmishes occurred along the remote and often poorly defined borders between the two rival powers. These occurred in January 1935 and March 1936 but only involved a few troops on each side. Another clash took place between the river fleets of the Manchukuo Navy and the Soviet River Flotilla in June 1937. The first large-scale conflict between Soviet units of the Far Eastern Army and Japanese troops of the Kwangtung Army occurred in the east of Manchukuo in the Changkufeng region in July 1938. Fighting broke out after Soviet troops had encroached on Changkufeng Hill on the Korean–Soviet–Manchurian border. Even though the 7,300 Japanese, equipped with 37 artillery pieces, had chosen to ignore this infringement on their territory, a further advance by Soviet troops 2 weeks later onto Shatsaofeng Hill led to fighting. A Japanese night attack forced back the Soviet unit occupying both hills, which were occupied by the Imperial Army. This was followed by 8 days of heavy bombardment by Soviet artillery and bombers which killed 526 Japanese. Soviet forces were made up of 23,000 troops, 345 tanks and 237 artillery pieces. When a ceasefire was arranged the Japanese could claim a victory but soon fighting was to break out on the other side of Manchukuo.

This larger scale campaign was fought over a disputed zone to the north of the border between the MPR and Manchukuo. Known as the Nomonhan Incident from the name of the nearest town in the disputed region, the war was effectively a proxy war. This was because Manchukuo was a puppet state of Japan and the MPR was a client state of the Soviet Union. Beginning on 11 May, the fighting took the form of small-scale skirmishes which gradually escalated into raids and counter raids across the borders. Japanese forces in the region totalled 76,000 men, 73 tanks, 64 tankettes, 300 artillery pieces and about 40,000 Manchukuoan troops. Facing them were 74,000 Soviet troops, 550 tanks, 450 armoured cars and several divisions of Mongolian cavalry. After two-and-a-half months of fighting the Japanese decided to launch an offensive, which began on 25 July. Japanese attacks soon ground to a halt as they faced superior Russian tanks, artillery and air support. The Japanese suffered heavy casualties, the 23rd Division incurring 73 per cent losses during the battle. Many of the Japanese wounded died needlessly as the first-aid treatment of their wounds was primitive.

After the offensive stalled, the Japanese and the Soviets rested for a few weeks while their respective air arms fought dog fights over the steppes. During this lull in the fighting the Soviet forces were heavily reinforced by more troops, tanks and artillery. This meant that when the Soviet forces launched their own large-scale offensive on 20 August they had a major advantage over the weary Japanese. The Soviet offensive was far more successful than that of the Japanese and the Imperial Army was soon encircled and largely destroyed by the Soviet forces. Poorer quality tanks were one of the major problems for the Japanese who found themselves outgunned in most tank on tank engagements. By the time the Soviet offensive ended on 31 August the Japanese had lost 8,440 dead and 8,766 wounded as well as 42 of their tanks. The peace settlement between the Japanese and the Soviet Union was to last until the Manchurian Campaign of August 1945. Japan's resounding defeat came as a terrible shock to their formerly victorious officers and high command and caused a great deal of reflection. Poor tactics, inferior weaponry and bad organization had accentuated the advantage the Soviets already had. Plans to introduce more modern weaponry and equipment were speeded up as the Imperial Army prepared for their next conflict.

Japanese troops charge up a slope in the early days of the fighting between the Kwangtung Army and the Soviet Far Eastern Army in May 1939. By 1939 there were nine Japanese infantry divisions of the Kwangtung Army in the region, comprising 270,000 men, 200 tanks and 560 aircraft. They were faced by a possible 570,000 Soviet troops with over 4 times the number of tanks and armoured cars available. The conflict was largely unknown at the time as both combatants did not really want the outside world to know about it.

(**Opposite, above**) A machine-gun crew guarding an Imperial Army barracks in the deserts of Inner Mongolia. When the Japanese conquered all three provinces that made up the region of Inner Mongolia in 1937 they then shared a border with the MPR. The MPR was a client state of the Soviet Union and for the next few years minor border clashes took place on a regular basis. After a small-scale war broke out in the Changkufeng border region in Eastern Manchukuo in 1938 another larger conflict was inevitable between the Japanese and the Soviet Union.

(**Opposite, below**) Two Japanese artillery spotters look out over a Mongolian village on the border between the Manchukuoan empire and the MPR. The disputed zone between the two client states of Japan and the Soviet Union was in Manchukuoan territory but was claimed by the MPR. As the Soviet forces supporting the MPR and the Japanese forces alongside their Manchukuoan allies built up their presence in the border region in 1939 war had to follow. Although soldiers of the Mongolian People's Army and of the Manchukuoan Army were to take part in the coming war, most of the fighting was done by Soviet and Japanese troops.

(**Above**) Japanese troops look out across the open plains of Manchuria as the build-up of military forces on either side of the border between Manchukuo and the MPR accelerates. In May 1939 the Japanese had the 5th and 4th armies of the Kwangtung Army in Manchukuo and although this force was formidable, they were faced by Soviet forces at least twice their strength. In addition the Soviets had more planes, tanks and artillery at their disposal with plenty of reinforcements available if necessary.

(**Opposite, above**) A Japanese platoon pose proudly with various items of Soviet army weaponry and equipment captured in an engagement. Their haul includes a Soviet DT tank machine gun which has been dismounted for use as an infantry gun. Behind the man with the machine gun another soldier rather bizarrely sports a captured Soviet army gas mask. On the right-hand side of the photograph are a couple of tank crewmen wearing overalls with their M32 helmets. In the centre of the group a soldier wears spectacles, which was a common sight in the army with the higher level of short-sightedness, or 'myopia', in the Japanese population. When the war began recruits with myopia were classed as B1 and were generally not enlisted. As the war intensified after 1941 classes B1–B3 were enlisted as the high level of casualties led to a reduction in recruiting standards.

(**Opposite, below**) A Japanese infantry unit takes up position on the side of a hill in the Nomonhan region supported by two Type 89 tanks. The Type 89, which had been introduced into service from 1929, was a slow tank with a maximum speed of 15mph. When facing Soviet medium tanks in 1939 it had a similar armament and armoured protection but its speed was far inferior. There were thirty-four Type 89s in service during the war with the Soviets and these formed the backbone of the Japanese armoured force.

(**Above**) The crew of a Soviet BT-5 medium tank surrender to a Japanese officer by waving a white cloth during the Nomonhan fighting in July 1939. Although the BT-5 was superior in speed to the Japanese tanks it encountered in 1939, many were destroyed or taken during the war. Some Soviet tanks were captured by often suicidal attacks mounted by the Japanese, who clambered aboard them and prised open hatches or shot through viewing slits. Such actions were often carried out while under fire from other Soviet tanks and supporting infantry with fatal results.

(**Opposite, above**) A Type 92 heavy machine-gun crew wait for a Soviet attack in a camouflaged post outside a Mongolian village. The Japanese were usually experts in taking advantage of any natural cover afforded by the terrain they were fighting in. However, during the Nomonhan Campaign this was not usually available and dug-in positions like this were the best option. Some Japanese officers criticized their men's skill in digging positions during the fighting with one commenting that his men's foxholes were not as deep as those of their Soviet adversaries.

(**Opposite, below**) A Japanese infantry unit moves cautiously across the open Mongolian steppe towards two destroyed Soviet armoured cars. These BA-10 armoured cars would have made a very useful addition to the Japanese inventory if they had been repairable. Although the Japanese recovered many Soviet tanks, armoured cars and artillery pieces from the battlefield, they do not appear to have used them in action.

(**Above**) This motorized unit has halted for a rest break during an advance across the Mongolian plains. Amongst the vehicles in use are a Hiziri 1.5-ton truck at the front of the column of trucks and at the rear a Toyota 4 x 2 1.5-ton truck. The staff cars are Nissan sedans which were the most common type used in the 1930s by the Imperial Army. Several of the unit's drivers have face masks on to protect them against the dust thrown up by the vehicles in the dry desert conditions.

(**Opposite, above**) A Japanese-produced Isuzu 6 x 4 1.5-ton truck is dragged by ropes out of a quagmire as the road across the Mongolian steppes turns to mud. The rest of the motorized column is waiting for this truck to be freed before they can continue their advance. First built in 1934, by 1939 the Isuzu was one of the workhorses of the Imperial Army and continued in service until 1945. Behind the Isuzu appears to be a Nissan sedan car which is being used as a staff car by the transport unit.

(**Opposite, below**) Japanese trucks move across the Mongolian steppes during the Imperial Army's advance in early July 1939. The huge distances travelled by both sides during the campaign meant that motor transport was vital. Equipment and uniforms are piled high on the truck, while its human cargo cling on for dear life. Trucks were also used to transport mobile infantry and special anti-tank teams into battle, although these were easy targets for Soviet tanks and artillery.

北境第一線

This propaganda postcard symbolizes the Japanese struggle against adversity in its wars in Northern China and Manchuria. The soldier proudly holds the Japanese flag aloft over another snow-covered outpost of the newly conquered regions of China. Japanese soldiers had spent most of their service on the Chinese mainland since the early twentieth century, fighting in the continent's extreme conditions. They were soon to be faced with adverse conditions at the other extreme as the Imperial Army turned its face southwards for new conquests in South-East Asia.

(**Opposite, above**) The crew of a Type 94 37mm anti-tank gun has prepared a defensive position for their gun on the Mongolian steppe. This model of gun was officially described in reports as a 'rapid fire gun' in an attempt to confuse the enemy about its true role. Type 94s were, like 37mms in service with other nations, becoming less effective by 1939 as the tanks they opposed got heavier. This being said, the Type 94 was described as highly accurate and was well liked by its crews.

(**Opposite, below**) Soldiers look out across the open plains of the Mongolian steppe as their officer points towards the horizon. In the confused fighting that took place in 1939 units would often become isolated, especially if they lost their transport. By the look of their weaponry these men may well be dismounted cavalry as they are armed with Type 44 carbines. The Type 44 introduced in 1911 was commonly known as the Kiju and was also used on occasion by some infantry.

(**Opposite, above**) The crew of a Japanese Model 90 (1930) 75mm gun fire their gun from their dug-in position towards a Soviet target in the summer of 1939. This particular model of the gun, which was introduced in 1936, has pneumatic tyres on its high-speed carriage. Most artillery pieces used by the Japanese during the Nomonhan conflict were of an earlier era.

(**Opposite, below**) Japanese and Soviet officers meet during one of the peace discussions between the two sides at the end of the 1939 campaign in September. The two officers sat in the centre are General Potapov and Major General Fujimoto Tetsukuma. By the end of the month a ceasefire had been agreed and an exchange of prisoners took place. However, for the Japanese POWs a bleak welcome awaited them when they returned to Japan. The shame of having surrendered to the Soviet army meant that many chose suicide to avoid embarrassing their families.

(**Above**) In a typical propaganda photograph of 1940 these sumo wrestlers are being given arms drill in a break from their conventional training. Presumably, the intention is to show that all members of Japanese society were ready to defend the empire against any enemy. The wrestlers are armed with older type rifles, although it is doubtful if they were expected to serve in even a second line role.

A tank unit parades down one of the main streets in the Japanese capital Tokyo in the late 1930s. Most of the tanks are Type 97 CHI-Hs, which was selected for mass production by Mitsubishi in 1937. It was based on the Type 95 light tank, one of which can be seen on the left-hand side of the photograph. It had a 47mm main armament rather than the 37mm of the Type 95 and an extra crewman as well as thicker armour. Type 97s were also less cramped than the Type 95 and had a two-man turret instead of the one-man in the lighter tank.

A unit of the Kwangtung Army hauls an infantry gun aboard a truck during a military manoeuvre in 1940. The men are wearing a white band around their helmets to signify which army they belong to during the mock battle. After its heavy defeat in the Nomonhan Campaign of 1939, the Kwangtung Army spent the 1940–5 period trying to rebuild itself. The gun is a Model 41 75mm, which was lightweight and so could be manhandled in the manner seen here.

Chapter Six

Japan Strikes South – Hong Kong and Malaya

Japan's conquests in China since 1931 and the atrocities committed there by its army had met with criticism from Europe and the USA throughout the 1930s. When Japan left the League of Nations in 1933 it was obvious that diplomatic pressure alone would not be able to force its military to end their aggression in China. Unofficial embargoes were introduced in the late 1930s which weakened an already fragile Japanese economy and caused outrage in Japan. Any criticism of Japan's policies in China was ignored by the Imperial Army, while the civilian population were powerless to change the situation. Within the Japanese military establishment there had long been an argument to continue its conquests on the Asian mainland or to 'Strike South' into South-East Asia. In Japan's sights were French Indo-China, British Malaya, the large naval base at Singapore and Burma as well as the Philippines under USA protection and Thailand.

Most of the resources the Japanese sought were to be found in the European ruled colonies of South-East Asia and the Pacific. There was oil in the Dutch East Indies and rubber in British-ruled Malaya. There was also sources of tin, nickel, bauxite and rice, all of which were desperately needed in Japan. For decades the Japanese had been laying the groundwork for a possible invasion of the territories of the region, Malaya and the Dutch East Indies being their primary targets. Any conquest of these territories would need to be accompanied by Japanese domination of the Pacific. This would involve going to war with the British empire and the USA, which had strategic interests in the Philippines.

To dominate the Pacific the Japanese Imperial Fleet would have to destroy British, US and Dutch naval power. If this was successful the Japanese could then conquer any British, Dutch or US controlled territory. In preparation for their coming offensive in South-East Asia the Japanese had gained bases in the Vichy controlled French Indo-China in 1940 and 1941. They also pressured Thailand through diplomatic and military means into allowing access through their territory across the border into Malaya when the offensive began. The USA introduced a series of crippling embargoes on Japan in 1940 and 1941 and froze their assets in July 1941. At the same time the Dutch East Indies refused to supply the Japanese with the strategic materials, including oil, that they demanded. This led the Imperial Armed Forces to move their plans to strike in the Pacific forward before the oil shortage hit them hard.

The Imperial Navy's air attack on the US Pacific Fleet at Pearl Harbor on 7 December 1941 was immediately followed by a series of land offensives. Malaya was invaded by the Imperial 21st Army on 8 December and after crushing British forces in the North began to advance down the peninsula. At the same time the Japanese invaded the British Crown Colony of Hong Kong in South China with 50,000 men of the 23rd Army. Hong Kong's poorly armed 12,000-man garrison was overrun after heavy fighting on Christmas Day 1941. Meanwhile, the Japanese were continuing their offensive down the coastlines of the Malay Peninsula with 120 armoured vehicles and 400 artillery pieces. They also had total air superiority and employed 459 Army Air Force planes and 158 navy planes in the fighting. The campaign was essentially a fighting retreat by the British army with attempts made at various points to stop the Imperial Army's advance. By February the Japanese were approaching the naval base of Singapore and the remaining British and Common-wealth troops withdrew from the mainland onto the island. When Singapore fell on 15 February the 85,000-man British garrison came into Japanese hands. Described as 'Japan's Greatest Victory and Britain's Greatest Defeat', the capture of Singapore was a major blow to the British war effort. At the same time it was to prove the zenith of Japan's campaign in South-East Asia, although it was not won without cost. The Japanese losses during the Malayan Campaign totalled 9,600, of which 3,500 were killed and 6,100 wounded. Meanwhile, other Japanese armies were winning victories elsewhere in South-East Asia and the Pacific resulting in more humiliations for Britain, the USA and the Dutch.

(**Opposite, above**) Japanese and Vichy French officers smile for the cameras during local negotiations for the taking over of a military base by the Imperial Army in 1940. After the fall of France in June 1940 the Japanese seized the opportunity to put pressure on the newly installed pro-German Vichy government. The Vichy government had been allowed to keep control of Indo-China but the Japanese wanted to use the territory that bordered Burma as a jumping off point for their planned invasion. Control of Indo-China would also allow the Imperial Army to advance through a subdued Thailand into Northern Malaya.

(**Opposite, below**) Imperial Army troops of the 5th Division under the command of General Akihito Nakamura drag their Type 41 75mm regimental gun through the streets of Hanoi in September 1940. On 25 September Japanese forces took Hanoi and the Northern Vietnamese port of Haiphong under their control. Unusually, the artillerymen are having to move their gun to a new position in the city centre themselves. Crew members are smartly turned out in tropical uniform and all are wearing the 2nd pattern cork sun helmet. This hat was similar in shape to the M32 steel helmet, whereas the 1st pattern was shaped like a traditional pith helmet.

Japanese troops cycle over a railway bridge into the Southern Vietnamese city of Saigon in July 1941. The Japanese forced the Vichy governor of Indo-China, Admiral Decoux, to accept the takeover of three airfields and agree to the garrisoning of their troops in strategic parts of the territory in late 1940. In 1941 the last of the Japanese demands were met by the Vichy government and this meant the Japanese could move their troops into any part of Indo-China. Although this was officially in agreement with the Vichy government, in reality the Japanese now had total control of Vietnam.

This much-produced 'Rise of Asia' propaganda poster represents the Japanese aim of uniting a newly 'liberated' Asia under their protection. The soldier is shown symbolically breaking the chains from the Asian population, the links featuring the letters A, B and D. These signify Australia, British, Dutch and America, the Allied nations that faced the Japanese onslaught beginning in December 1941. At his feet are the prone figures of Uncle Sam and Churchill to further emphasize Asia's enemies in the eyes of the Japanese.

Japanese army officers hold a conference at the customs office on the Kowloon & District Railway near Hong Kong. The British colony, garrisoned by 11,848 men, fell after an 18-day battle on Christmas Day 1941. Its commander, Major General Maltby, ordered the troops to lay down their arms at 15.30 on the 25th. Fighting continued until the next day in certain areas and when the Japanese entered the city they committed a series of outrages against the garrison and 1,750,000 civilian population. The Japanese heavy losses totalled 2,754 during the battle and this was perhaps one reason, but not an excuse for, the Imperial Army's behaviour.

(**Opposite, above**) Soldiers of the 38th Imperial Division march into Hong Kong from the leased territories on the Chinese mainland. The Japanese had numerical and materiel superiority over the garrison defending the British colony as well as total air superiority. The first attacks on the borders of the colony began in the hours after the strike on Pearl Harbor on 8 December. British, Canadian and other troops who made up the defenders were spread thinly as Hong Kong was threatened on all sides by the Japanese.

(**Opposite, below**) A unit of Naval Landing Troops move through Kavieng on the island of New Ireland, part of the Bismark Archipelago, on 23 January 1942. Once the island had been taken it was converted into an air and naval base by the Imperial Navy. The Japanese sent a 5,000-strong force to capture New Britain, New Ireland and Bougainville, which were all part of the Solomon Islands.

(**Above**) Troops move at speed across a hastily made wooden bridge over a fast-flowing stream in Malaya. The structure is being held together by the engineers who have built it. These assault bridges were built to a specific design and were vital to the speedy advance of the army in 1941–2. Presumably the wooden sections of the bridge would be transported, when possible, to build the next one in the advance, while a more permanent one would replace it if necessary. Each Japanese infantry division had a regiment of engineers divided into three companies of 250 men each.

A heavily camouflaged Japanese Model 94 light tank waits in the Malayan jungle to go into action after its crew have piled foliage on it. The Model 94 was a two-man tankette with a small machine-gun armed turret and was usually used for reconnaissance and infantry support. Its commander is wearing summer overalls and the summer version of the crash helmet without the fur lining.

The cover image of an illustrated Japanese news magazine which features a sergeant major in Malaya cleaning his 1935 NCO pattern sword ready to go into action. The sergeant is wearing typical tropical uniform with shirt, shorts and field cap with a sun neck flap. Swords were carried by most officers and the more wealthy would often bring their own family heirlooms which had been passed down to them.

This photograph has previously been claimed to show Japanese troops in the Burmese, New Guinea or Philippines jungle. It was, however, originally taken from a news magazine and the original caption stated that these troops were in Malaya in early 1942. The image shows the typical conditions that the Japanese Imperial Army faced on all fronts during their victorious advance through South-East Asia. In the dense jungle small units like this would often not see their enemy until they were a few yards or even feet away.

General Yamashita is featured on the cover of the *Shashin Shuho* illustrated magazine in February 1942. Yamashita's triumph in capturing Singapore in seventy days with limited resources made him a hero to the Japanese population. This popularity, however, made him a potential rival to Japanese Prime Minister Tojo, who engineered his transfer to Manchuria later in the year. After being brought back from virtual exile to defend the Philippines in 1944 he was tried and executed for war crimes in Manila in 1946. Even at the time there were many that said that Yamashita was a scapegoat for other more guilty officers. It was said that his misfortune was to hold such a high rank that he was't informed of the atrocities being committed in his name.

(**Opposite, above**) Not everything went the Japanese army's way during their 'procession' through Malaya and this highly-publicized ambush was covered in the British press. In this action a patrol of Japanese Type 95 tanks was destroyed by the 2-pounder guns of an Australian battery at Johore. A well-prepared roadblock had been turned into an ambush position that the overconfident Japanese tankers fell into. Despite the odd setback, the Japanese advance moved on relentlessly and the loss of a few tanks did not deflect them from their final objective.

(**Above**) General Yamashita Tomoyuki, the commander of the 25th Army in Malaya, studies a map in the final days before the fall of Singapore on 15 February 1942. His victory won him the title 'Tiger of Malaya' and earned him the adoration of the Japanese population. When the Imperial Army took Singapore their manpower and materiel resources were stretched to the limit. The force that attacked the fortress was made up of sixteen front-line and five reserve battalions of varying quality. Troops had to be transported across the causeway between mainland Malaya and Singapore with only 13,000 getting across in the first 24 hours of the battle.

Japanese troops haul their 75mm gun over a bank in the Malayan jungle as the Imperial Army's advance continues. The weapon is a Model 94 mountain gun, the standard pack howitzer of the Imperial Army. As result of the difficult terrain in Malaya the invading army included nine companies of engineers which followed behind the front-line troops. Their first task was to restore any bridges destroyed by the retreating British forces and then repair railways and build airfields.

Imperial Army bicycle troops peddle down a road in Malaya. As well as being used along roads and tracks, the Japanese soldier would carry this unconventional mode of transport through jungle to ride whenever possible. The 'peddling army' was described as Japan's secret weapon in its campaign in Malaya and was part of the Japanese policy of adapting to whatever environment they faced. Although many Japanese were familiar with bicycles, others would have had to be given basic training in their use.

These Japanese cyclists have halted during their southwards advance, their bicycles laden with kit and other equipment. Most cycles used during the Malayan Campaign were the military model which was built on a robust and simple frame with large wheels. Others would have been picked up along the way to increase the number of troops who could advance at the pace of their mounted comrades. The Japanese also had a handcart which was designed to be pulled behind the army bicycle and could carry a few men's kit.

A Japanese soldier takes a much-needed water break during the advance down the Malay Peninsula. The Imperial Army soldier was soon regarded as some kind of superman by his enemy. One myth is that they were at home in the jungle of Malaya but the truth is that it was as alien an environment as it was to the Commonwealth troops. In fact, most soldiers did not even know the meaning of the word 'jungle' and they had never seen it until they landed in Malaya.

(**Opposite, above**) Type 97 medium tanks rumble down Orchard Street after the capture of the island base of Singapore. In total the Japanese had fifty-six Type 97 tanks in service during the Malayan Campaign, of which thirty-one were from the 1st Tank Regiment and twenty-five from the 6th Regiment. British and Australian troops had little weaponry to counter these tanks as they withdrew down the Malay Peninsula. Fortunately for the Imperial Army the Allied nations did not have tanks present in the theatre that could have fought this model.

(**Opposite, below**) Proud Japanese soldiers march past the General Post Office in the centre of Singapore dressed in a variety of tropical uniform. This photograph illustrates well the Japanese soldiers' complete disregard for smartness when in the front line. Although most of the troops are wearing shirt and breeches, the man in the centre is only wearing his undershirt. After having fought such a difficult campaign due to the terrain they had advanced through they were ready for a rest. Some units, however, were almost immediately sent to fight in other theatres of the war.

Japanese troops drag in a nervous-looking British or Australian prisoner during their advance through Malaya. On some occasions Allied prisoners were quietly executed instead of being handed over to the correct authorities. If they survived this initial period of captivity they faced a grim future in the poorly run POW camps. Any Indian troops captured by the Japanese were kept apart from their former comrades in an attempt to turn them into collaborators.

Following the fall of Singapore British troops stand at the mercy of their captors, who gather around their fearful prisoners. Japanese troops had no respect for any soldier who chose not to fight to the death and this disdain for their captives was to lead in many cases to their mistreatment. Unfortunately, taller prisoners appear to have been subjected to particularly poor treatment perhaps due to a subconscious inferiority complex on the part of their captors. The victorious Japanese, however, had everything to be confident about having completely humiliated their enemy during the fighting.

Japanese troops come ashore from rowing boats at Natunna on the north-western coast of Borneo in December 1941. In the early stages of the Japanese takeover of the island they seized strategic targets in the British territories of Sarawak and British Borneo. The rest of Borneo, which was ruled by the Dutch, was conquered in a series of amphibious landings from 11 January to 10 February 1942. Most of the oilfields that had been the target of the Japanese offensive were put out of action by the defenders.

Chapter Seven

The Offensive Continues – Burma, Philippines and the Dutch East Indies

(1941–2)

While the Japanese were advancing through Malaya their comrades in the 15th Imperial Army moved from Northern Thailand into Southern Burma. The 15th Army had taken control of Thailand on 8 December 1941 and used the newly occupied country as a jumping off point for their invasion of Burma. Made up of the 55th and 33rd divisions and the 14th Tank Regiment, the 15th Army entered Burma on 14 December and had captured Rangoon by 8 March. Facing them were the British Burma Army, made up of two Indian divisions from the rapidly expanding British Indian Army. In addition, there were veterans from the 8th Army in North Africa, with M3 light tanks, and some Chinese Nationalist divisions. After taking Southern Burma the Japanese began an advance northwards chasing the British forces ahead of them. Although there was heavy resistance to the Japanese, their advance continued until by the end of May 1942 they had pushed the British army and some Chinese forces across the border into India. Other Chinese divisions had retreated back into Yunnan province having lost all their eighty tanks in the campaign. It had been a hard-fought campaign in difficult terrain for the Japanese, who lost 4,500 casualties.

Japan's invasion of the Philippines had begun immediately after the attack on Pearl Harbor, the first troops landing on the island of Luzon on 12 December. The invasion involved the 57,000-strong 14th Imperial Army, which made further landings on Luzon and the other large Philippines island of Mindanao throughout December. They were faced by a sizeable but largely irregular poorly armed and trained Filipino army which was 140,000 strong and reinforced by 31,000 regular Filipino and US troops. Between January and April the Filipino and US forces on Luzon were gradually forced by the Japanese into the Bataan Peninsula, where 78,000 of them surrendered on 9 April. The last US and Filipino troops then withdrew into the Fortress of

Corregidor in Manila Bay, where they held out for almost a month before surrendering on 6 May. The campaign had been a disaster for the USA but the Japanese won the victory while sustaining only 1,900 dead.

For the Japanese the main prize in their conquest of South-East Asia was the enormous territory of the Dutch East Indies, which included the large islands of Java, Sumatra and Borneo as well as 17,000 other smaller islands. The area had large oil fields and other natural resources which made it very attractive to the Japanese. The Dutch East Indies was defended by its 65,000-strong Dutch East Indies Army (KNIL), which was made up largely of native troops. Although the KNIL had been reinforced by some British and Australian troops, it could only offer brief resistance to the invaders. On 26 February the Imperial Navy had defeated a hastily organized combined Dutch, Australian, US and British fleet in the Battle of the Java Sea. This victory immediately gave the Japanese the opportunity of sending their invasion force to invade the Dutch East Indies. Three Japanese divisions landed on the Dutch East Indies island of Java on 28 February 1942. In just over a week the Dutch were forced to surrender with the defeat of the KNIL completed by 8 March.

Apart from Malaya, Burma, the Philippines and the Dutch East Indies other Japanese conquests included the island of Borneo. Borneo was divided between the British and Dutch with Sarawak and Brunei under British rule and Dutch Borneo comprising the southern half of the territory. It was defended by a total of 3,000 Dutch, Indian and local British forces during a campaign that lasted from December 1941 to March 1942. The Imperial 37th Army was given the responsibility of taking the island, which it eventually succeeded in doing by early March.

By the time the Japanese offensive in South-East Asia and the Pacific had come to an end the Imperial Army and Navy had taken all their objectives. These included the US pacific islands of Wake, taken on 24 December 1941, the Marshall Islands, the Solomon Islands and Northern New Guinea. Japan's spectacular victories now gave them a major problem as their offensive campaign turned into a defensive campaign. Their completely overstretched forces now had to fight to defend their newly won empire from the Allies.

(**Above**) Japanese Imperial troops present arms on the border between Thailand and Burma as they prepare to invade the British territory in January 1942. The invasion of Burma was really only designed to protect the flanks of the more important Japanese advances in Malaya and the Dutch East Indies. Imperial Army plans called for the rapid takeover of the Southern Burma followed by the destruction of British Indian forces before they could retire northwards.

(**Opposite, above**) Artillerymen manhandle the barrel of a light gun through the Burmese jungle during the 1942 campaign. They are cradling the barrel on a tree branch as well as taking some of the weight by hand. Although the average Japanese soldier was small in stature, he was usually wiry and at least in the early years of the war had a strong physique. The majority of recruits were from rural backgrounds and had been hardened by years of labouring in the fields before joining the army.

(**Opposite, below**) Two soldiers and an officer move forward at the double across open ground during the Burmese Campaign in 1942. All three of the men are wearing tropical uniforms with light cotton shirts and breeches, while the two privates wear the M32 steel helmet. The officer has the 2nd pattern cork sun helmet and carries a typical *shin-gunto* sword in his hand. He is also armed with an automatic pistol in its holster which could be the Type 14 or the Type 94. Both automatic pistols in service with the Imperial Army were poor designs but were all that was available to most officers.

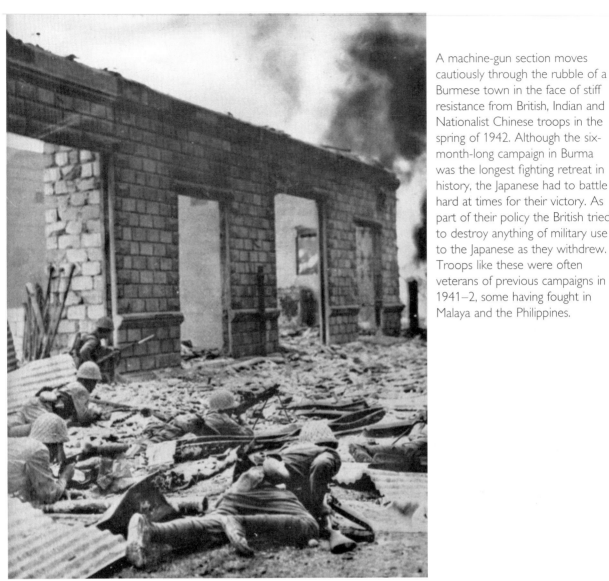

A machine-gun section moves cautiously through the rubble of a Burmese town in the face of stiff resistance from British, Indian and Nationalist Chinese troops in the spring of 1942. Although the six-month-long campaign in Burma was the longest fighting retreat in history, the Japanese had to battle hard at times for their victory. As part of their policy the British tried to destroy anything of military use to the Japanese as they withdrew. Troops like these were often veterans of previous campaigns in 1941–2, some having fought in Malaya and the Philippines.

(**Opposite, above**) General Renya Mutaguchi, the 54-year-old commander of the 18th Division in Burma, chats with an officer during the victorious campaign in 1942. Mutaguchi had served in Malaya, where he was wounded in the shoulder, and in the Philippines before being sent to Burma. The general went on to command the 15th Army in Burma and was in charge of the 1944 offensive against Imphal. After the disastrous failure of the Imphal offensive which he had supported Mutaguchi was forcibly retired. He survived the war and, unusually for high-ranking officers of the Imperial Army in 1941–5, lived into old age.

(**Opposite, below**) Fast-moving Type 95 HA-GO light tanks travel in column along a dirt road during the Burma Campaign in May 1942. At 28mph, the Type 95 was reasonably fast but it had light armour which was only resistant against small-arms fire. As the main role of the tank was seen as reconnaissance, the lack of radios in most of the Type 95s was a major problem. Its main armament was the 37mm Type 94 gun which was becoming obsolete by 1942, and although it had two machine guns the rear offset one was not that useful. Even with all these drawbacks the Type 95 served the Imperial Army until 1945 and was the most produced model in service. In total 1,164 were manufactured by Mitsubishi and another 150 or so at smaller plants.

An artillery unit of the 33rd Division pulls its Type 41 47mm anti-tank gun across a river during the advance though Burma in 1942. The bridge the gun is crossing looks like it has been simply constructed but is obviously strong enough to take the unit's overloaded truck. Piled into the back of the lorry appears to be the crew's equipment as well as ammunition for the gun. Type 41s were a new weapon for the Imperial Army, having been introduced into service a few months before. During the campaign the 33rd Division fought 34 battles in 127 days and suffered heavy casualties in the process.

In a typical example of Japanese improvisation in jungle fighting this machine-gun unit in Burma in 1942 has built a wooden firing platform for their Type 3. The two crewmen are, however, very exposed to enemy fire, while their comrades take cover in the bushes. In the early years of the Pacific War the Japanese soldier earned a reputation not only for bravery but also for ingenuity in battle. All the troops are wearing typical tropical uniforms with canvas covers on their M32 steel helmets.

During the advance through Burma in early 1942 this Japanese unit have conscripted locals and their elephants to transport themselves and their equipment. The unit's kit has been piled onto the platforms on top of the elephants, while one soldiers also gets a lift. His comrades, along with civilian porters, follow in the distance, while the soldier at the front of the column is armed with a Type 44 carbine.

A colour party of a Japanese Naval Landing Force unit looks out from a hill top as US and Philippines forces withdraw in the Bataan Peninsula in January 1942. As the Allied troops retreated into Bataan they were kept under a steady bombardment by Japanese land and naval forces. Naval Landing Forces generally wore a green uniform with navy insignia on their helmets and sleeves. Flags carried by the Naval Landing Forces were distinguished by having an offset red sun and rays which were not seen on army standards.

Lieutenant General Homma relaxes after his victory over the US and Philippines armies in May 1942. Homma was a career officer who had served for many years as a military attaché in London and had an understanding of the Western way of fighting. He was worried about Japan's chances in a war against the USA but loyally served his emperor as commander of the 14th Army. His failure to clear some of the Philippines islands according to schedule lost him favour with the high command in Tokyo. For the rest of the Pacific War he did not receive an operational command but was executed in 1946 for crimes committed by his troops.

The two-man crew of a Type 97 20mm automatic gun in the Philippines. Designed primarily as an anti-tank weapon, it was introduced in 1937 and first used against Soviet armour in the Nomonhan Incident in 1939. The magazine held seven rounds of standard or High Explosive type and was operated, as seen here, by a two-man crew. Officially the Type 97 had an eight-man crew to transport and set it up, but once in place it needed only a firer and a loader, who also steadied its bipod during firing. It was never in widespread use with the Imperial Army and only 400 were produced according to official figures.

This tough-looking soldier stands proudly in the ruins of Manila with the Balanga Cathedral in the background. The Philippines invasion force was made up of the 14th Army and only had a strength of 57,000 men. They were faced by the Philippines Commonwealth Army of 109,000 men and 31,000 US troops. However, most of the Filipino soldiers were poorly armed as the military budget for the defence of the Philippines was totally inadequate.

Triumphant Japanese soldiers celebrate with a enthusiastic banzai having taken another strongpoint in their advance through the Philippines. The heady days of victory that began in December 1941 were to continue until the final defeat of the Allied armies in Burma in May 1942. Japan's creation of a Greater East Asia Co-Prosperity Sphere, or *Daitoa Kyoueiken*, was supposed to free the downtrodden peoples of Burma, the Philippines, Malaya and the rest of Asia. In reality most Asian people who now fell under their rule soon realized that they had only swapped one type of colonial rule for another.

A flamethrower team attack one of the pillboxes on the US-held Fortress of Corregidor in May 1942. The flamethrower is a Model 93, which along with the slightly modified Model 100 was the standard type used by the Imperial Army throughout the war. It could send a 27m flame out for up to 12 seconds which was created by igniting mixed pressured nitrogen and fuel. In this obviously posed photograph the operator is exposing himself, while his comrades shelter behind the slope.

(**Above**) Soldiers standing on the gun positions of the Fortress of Corregidor after its fall on 6 May 1942. Built into the solid rock of the island off the coast of Bataan, Corregidor and its 15,000-strong garrison was the last US outpost in the Philippines to hold out. Japanese troops of the 4th Division had landed on the island fortress the day before but had initially suffered heavy casualties.

(**Opposite page**) A lone Japanese soldier stands looking out over a burning village during the battle for the Dutch East Indies island of Java. After Japan declared war on the Dutch government in exile the fate of the poorly defended and resource-rich islands was sealed. Although the KNIL was numerically strong, the majority of its troops were natives, many of who were regarded by the Dutch as unreliable. The KNIL was really an old-fashioned colonial army with some modern armoured vehicles, artillery and aircraft. The numerous islands that made up the Dutch East Indies fell in a three-month campaign, which was half the time that the Japanese high command had expected.

A column of Imperial Army troops march down a jungle road as curious natives of a Dutch East Indies island look on. Although some peoples of South-East Asia saw the Japanese as fellow Asian liberators from colonial rule, most were soon to become disillusioned. These soldiers are carrying all their kit in the haversacks on their backs and have the sun flap of their field caps to protect their necks. The officer carrying the unit's standard is wearing a visibly smarter and darker khaki uniform and white parade gloves.

(**Opposite, above**) Naval Landing Troops come ashore on an unknown Pacific Island as the Japanese navy continued to occupy outlying islands in 1942. As the Japanese offensive ground to a halt in the early summer any remaining islands within their sphere of control were occupied. Maintaining garrisons on some of the smaller and less strategic islands would prove impractical. Many of the smaller island garrisons were isolated almost from the moment they were occupied as the Imperial Navy struggled to supply them due to attrition on their shipping by the Allies.

(**Opposite, below**) In this highly posed photograph Naval Landing Troops come ashore on one of the Pacific Islands occupied by the Japanese in 1942. Many features of the uniforms, flags and equipment of the Naval Landing Forces can be seen here. In the foreground the seaman is firing the Type 89 50mm grenade launcher by pulling a pin. Range was altered by moving the firing pin up and down the barrel to change the force behind the grenade. On his and his comrades' helmets is the crossed anchor badge of the Naval Landing Force and on his sleeve is the red crossed anchor and cherry blossom rank badge for leading seaman 1st class. Standards carried by the seamen include the offset Naval Landing Force version of the Rising Sun flag as well as the Japanese national flag.

Chapter Eight

Burma
(1943–5)

After the conquest of Burma in May 1942 the Japanese spent the next year consolidating their political control of the country. In 1943 the pro-Japanese puppet government of Ba Maw was given nominal independence with its own 20,000-strong Burmese National Army. Of course, the Japanese Imperial Army maintained substantial forces in the newly 'independent' country and these had to throw back a limited Allied offensive in the Arakan region in West Burma in January 1943. This offensive was launched from its base in India by the untried British 14th Division, but after heavy fighting the demoralized Allies had to withdraw to their original positions. In another attempt to disrupt Japan's control of Burma the British launched a series of large-scale raids into Northern Burma. These Chindit operations were carried out by units that were to infiltrate behind Japanese lines and had received jungle training in preparation. The First Chindit Offensive of 1943, although only partially successful, had worried the Japanese Imperial Army command in Burma. They had learnt that the mountains and jungle of North-Western Burma were not the obstacle they had believed to Allied attacks from India. This realization led the Japanese commanders to conclude that the best way to defend Burma was to capture the British bases at Imphal and Kohima. From there the Imperial Army could then advance into India and ferment revolts to destabilize it. A large-scale offensive was planned for March 1944 by the Imperial Army's 15th Army with support from the 42,000-strong pro-Japanese Indian National Army.

A diversionary offensive, Operation Ha-Go, for the Imphal operation was launched by the 28th Imperial Army in February 1944 into the Arakan region of Western Burma. This offensive, however, soon ran out of steam when faced by stiff resistance from the 7th Indian Division and attacks from the Allied air force, which had gained air superiority over the Japanese. Ha-Go's main purpose had been to draw substantial British forces away from the Imphal defences in preparation for the Imphal Campaign but this did not happen.

Regardless of the failure of the earlier offensive, the larger Imphal Offensive, Operation U-Go, began on 15 March as three divisions advanced in nine large columns towards the British-held lines. Although the offensive made good process, tenuous supply lines meant that the Japanese soon began to run out of food and ammunition. The attackers were faced by 28,000 British and 30,000 Indian well-trained troops who held onto Imphal with the support of Allied aircraft, which had swept the Japanese planes from the sky. Local successes by the Japanese did include the crossing of the Burmese–Indian border by mixed Imperial Army and Indian National Army troops. The expected anti-British rebellion was never going to be a reality and the Indian National Army was soon pushed back into Burma.

In the meantime, the Imperial Army continued to fight desperately to try and capture Kohima and Imphal. Japanese troops were now starving, while their foes were well supplied most of the time by air drops. The Japanese plan to re-supply their soldiers from captured British stores was now shown to have been an unrealistic gamble. By the time the Japanese and their Indian allies began to withdraw they had lost 65,000 men and had resorted to eating grubs and grass as they tried to return to their own lines. The Imphal Offensive was a disaster for the Imperial Army in Burma and by mid-1945 there were only approximately 70,000 Japanese troops to defend against the coming Allied offensive. By July 1945 the remaining Japanese forces in Burma were desperately trying to break out and withdraw to neighbouring Malaya across the Sittang River. The orderly retreat soon became a hopeless rout with small units trying to slip past the surrounding British 14th Army. Most troops were killed in the attempt and during the July fighting the Japanese lost 11,500 men killed or captured while the Allied 14th Army lost a total of 96 men.

An Imperial Army unit receives its orders before going out on patrol into the Burmese jungle in 1943. Both the officer and his men have expertly camouflaged their shirts and headgear with foliage. By this stage in the war the Japanese had become adept at adapting to the terrain they fought in. Some camouflage items were made in Japan and shipped out to the army in the early stages of the Pacific War, however most troops had to improvise with whatever they could find.

(**Opposite page**) This photograph shows the kind of terrain that the Japanese soldier had to contend with during its campaigns in Burma. Moving heavy equipment up a sheer cliff was just as difficult for the Imperial Army soldiers as it was for their Allied foes. Many ordinary soldiers, however, came from rural backgrounds where they were accustomed to hard labour. They also knew that complaining to their officers was not a good idea and tended just to get on with the task they were given.

(**Above**) An artillery unit carries its mountain guns down a jungle track in Burma in 1943 having advanced up the hill they are now descending. They are carrying the dissembled parts of Type 92 70mm infantry guns distributing the 204kg payload between six men. The wheels, breech block, barrel, legs/spades and shield were each carried by one man, the strongest having a 68kg load. Additional crew members transported the shells for the gun in metal cases on their backs, each holding three rounds.

Japanese troops of the 18th Division struggle up a hill in the Shupii mountain range in Burma during an operation against a British Chindit force in March 1943. They are looking for Chindit forces who had launched Operation Longcloth in February having crossed the Chindwin River. In almost impossible terrain the British and Japanese played a game of 'cat and mouse' with both sides suffering terribly from the jungle conditions. The soldier at the head of the column has had to improvise a sling for his injured arm out of his *hinomaru* flag. *(George Forty)*

(**Opposite, above**) In a scene typical of the fighting in Burma in the period 1942–5 a unit of Japanese troops crosses a rickety wooden bridge over a flooded river in 1943. Unfortunately for the Imperial Army, most of the terrain of their newly won empire was almost totally inhospitable. These soldiers are lightly armed and seem relaxed so they are probably not expecting attacks from Allied regulars or Burmese irregulars. Their light cotton tropical uniforms were prone to rot in the extreme humidity of the Burmese jungle. In addition, they had to deal with tropical diseases, sores, leeches and poisonous snakes which challenged their image of being 'jungle supermen' to the limit.

(**Opposite, below**) During fighting in the Arakan region in the autumn of 1943 an infantry section of the Imperial Army advances through a mangrove swamp. They are preparing to face another Allied attack after the first Chindit operation ended with its surviving troops withdrawing back into India in June 1943. The men are wearing a mixture of tropical kit with the two soldiers in the foreground wearing light khaki shirts with the leading NCO having his rank bar on his sleeve. Their comrades have darker tropical shirts and one man has covered his pack with camouflage netting. *(George Forty)*

(**Opposite, above**) Although still masters of jungle warfare after their successful 1942 campaign, these troops advancing through the undergrowth in Arakan were by 1943 facing a more-determined and better trained enemy. The Allied soldier of 1943 was being given a new kind of jungle training which allowed the individual soldier to show initiative in combat. In contrast the Japanese, although hardy and courageous fighters, were constrained to some degree by their total obedience to their superior's orders. A Japanese soldier's main aim in jungle fighting was usually to get close to the enemy and then launch a bayonet charge. These soldiers' long bayonets on their Type 38 rifles were rather ungainly in the jungle but were perfect for a banzai charge.

(**Above**) Japanese troops sit on the bank of a river waiting to cross to the other side in a small boat during the Arakan Campaign of 1943. During the 1943 fighting in North-West Burma the many rivers and watercourses of the region were an obstacle for both the Imperial Army and Allied troops. Japanese troops were adept at building bamboo bridges over smaller rivers and streams but larger rivers had to be crossed by military or civilian boats. All the troops are suitably camouflaged for the jungle fighting ahead and have foliage tied to shirts, trousers and helmets with wire, string or netting.

(**Opposite, below**) This gun crew are firing their Type 41 mountain gun from a position on the Plain of Imphal in March 1944. In the coming offensive the Japanese artillery were to be outgunned 4 to 1 by the British. The Imphal Campaign was launched along a 150-mile front by nine large columns of troops taken from the 15th, 33rd and 31st divisions. Their advance was at first successful and the British bases at Imphal and Kohima were soon threatened. Kohima was besieged and the Japanese commander of the attacking force, General Sato, was ordered to take it by the emperor's birthday on 29 April. Instead, Sato withdrew his long-suffering and unsupplied soldiers, who had been reduced to eating slugs and grass.

Two soldiers from the 33rd Division move forward through a trench in Burma in May 1944. They are carrying mysterious equipment and the man in front appears to be wearing breathing apparatus. If he is wearing a gas mask, it suggests the use of chemical weapons which were not employed in South-East Asia during the war. It was reported, however, that chemical weapons were carried by some units as they advanced through Asia in 1941–2. Gas was used on about 2,000 occasions in China between 1931 and 1945 by the Japanese causing Chinese military and civilian casualties estimated at 100,000. The metal canister carried by the man at the rear is probably full of water for the troops in the front-line trenches as the container has a tap at the bottom. (*George Forty*)

(**Opposite, above**) A soldier of the 33rd Division shares the precious water from his canteen with a comrade during fighting in Burma in May 1944. Both soldiers are heavily camouflaged on their bodies with foliage and green material in an effort to merge into the jungle. The soldier holding the water bottle to be filled is armed with a Lee–Enfield .303 rifle captured from his British enemy. It is rare to see an Imperial Army soldier armed with British small arms, although they did make use of some captured Nationalist weapons in China.

(**Opposite, below**) Japanese Imperial troops march through the jungle in the early stages of the 1944 Imphal Campaign in March. The main aim of the campaign was to create a new defensive line in the mountains of Assam province in India. This would allow the Japanese to better defend Burma against the expected British, US and Chinese invasion when it came. The intention was that columns like this, carrying only a few days' supplies, would capture anything they needed from the British as they advanced. As well as the terrain, lack of food and disease, the Japanese also had to contend with the onset of the monsoon. When supplies ran out Japanese troops began to die from hunger as well as malaria and dysentery.

Soldiers of the Imperial 15th Army begin their long retreat from Burma in 1945, during which they were to suffer terribly from disease and hunger. With few supplies and heavily depleted numbers after the total defeat of their offensive in 1944, their commander, General Kimura, knew they had no chance of success. In total the 15th Army had 21,000 men in 4 divisions and little artillery or tanks to face the British Indian Army's nine strong divisions.

(**Opposite, above**) A mixed patrol of Imperial Army and Indian National Army troops are pictured on the Burmese border with India. The inclusion of thousands of Indian soldiers from the anti-British Indian National Army in the Imphal Campaign in 1944 was largely a propaganda exercise. Formed in Singapore in 1942 from British Indian Army POWs, the Indian National Army's aim was to free India by force of arms. Its leader, the veteran independence campaigner Subhas Chandra Bose, hoped that the Japanese would help him liberate his country. In reality the Indian National Army was given second-hand British rifles and cast-off uniforms and sent into action against Allied tanks and heavy artillery.

(**Opposite, below**) A Japanese patrol is welcomed, at least for propaganda purposes, by the population of a village on the Indian–Burmese border. The Imperial Army's Imphal Campaign had a secondary and totally unrealistic target. It was hoped that the Japanese and their Indian allies could take at least some British Indian territory on which they could establish an anti-British government. When the campaign lost its momentum its 'March On India' slogan sounded very much like a hollow boast. With few supplies and encountering some of the worst terrain in the world, the Imperial Army suffered terrible casualties before retreating to Burma.

This fine study of a Type 97 tankette driver was discovered with the body of the driver of the vehicle after the Duke of Wellington's Regiment captured it in Arakan in Burma in March 1945. The Type 97 was really an up-gunned version of the Type 94 tankette and only had 12mm of armour plating at most. Its 37mm main armament was totally inadequate and its top speed of 28mph was only 2 miles faster than the earlier tankette. Any Allied tanks it encountered in the last few months of the war would have soon destroyed it. The commander is wearing summer weight tank overalls and a cork crash helmet with goggles. *(RHQ, DWR, via Bill Norman)*

Chapter Nine

Japan on the Defensive in the Pacific (1942-5)

Japan's offensive operations in the Pacific continued into the summer of 1942 with the capture of several of the Aleutian Islands in the Northern Pacific in June. The Imperial Army and Navy had also landed on New Guinea, north of Australia in March 1942. New Guinea's strategic value was such that control of this huge island made it difficult for US supplies to reach Australia. Allied reasons for fighting for New Guinea was that it held the key to the southern approaches to and the eventual liberation of the Philippines. During the campaign Australian troops held the South-East New Guinea, while the Japanese 18th Army held the North and West. From mid-1942 until January 1943 a series of brutal offensives and counter-offensives took place over the inhospitable terrain, including high mountain ranges and impenetrable jungles. Losses were not only suffered on land and 3,664 men of the Japanese 51st Division became casualties when the ships taking them to New Guinea were sunk. As the Australians were reinforced the fighting on New Guinea turned into a stalemate and the 18th Army basically remained inactive for the rest of the war. Its troops were isolated and survived only by planting crops and rationing ammunition by avoiding encounters with the Australians. When the Japanese on New Guinea surrendered in 1945 there were only 13,000 of the original 140,000 men who had started the campaign.

The Japanese had also invaded the Solomon Islands to the east of New Guinea in early August 1942. Fighting for the Solomons centred on the islands of Guadalcanal, Bourgainville and New Georgia. On Guadalcanal the battle for the Japanese-built Henderson airfield was particularly fierce, but the fighting ended in February 1943 when the Japanese withdrew their forces from the island. US forces landed on New Georgia in June 1943 and on Bourgainville in November 1943 as the Allies took the war to the Japanese. In the Solomons they were faced by Japanese troops of the 8th Area Army who put up the usual fanatical resistance.

As Allied land and naval forces built up in Australia and the Pacific the future of the war was to be decided at sea. The Japanese Imperial Navy's defeat in the Battle of the Coral Sea in May and at Midway in early June 1942 by the US fleet effectively put them on the defensive for the rest of the war. Other naval battles in August 1942 (Savo Island) and March 1943 (Bismarck Sea) proved that the Japanese were now losing the war at sea in the Pacific. As more and more Japanese navy and merchant vessels were sunk by US ships, submarines and aircraft it became more and more difficult to supply their many Pacific garrisons. Although the total Japanese forces in the Pacific Theatre was still impressive during the 1942–4 period, they were reinforced when possible. Men and weaponry were stripped from units on the Chinese mainland and sent to the South-West Pacific. Most of the men, tanks, artillery and planes were to be sacrificed in usually pointless defences of islands between 1943 and 1945. A lot of the war materiel sent to the increasingly isolated garrisons on the Pacific Islands also ended up at the bottom of sea as the Imperial Navy lost the initiative at sea. The over extended supply lines to the more isolated Japanese-garrisoned islands meant that starvation rather than enemy action was the Imperial Army and Naval Landing Troops' main worry.

The US advance through the Pacific began in earnest with the capture of the Aleutian island of Attu in May 1943. This was followed later in the year by the landing of troops on Bourgainville in the Northern Solomon Islands and the capture of Tarawa in the Gilbert Islands in November. In 1944 the US westward offensive through the Pacific islands continued with the fall of the Marshall Islands, Kwajalein and Eniwetok and the Admiralty Islands in February. In June and July the Mariana Islands, Saipan and Guam fell to the US forces as well as the whole of the 30,000-strong garrison on Saipan, and a total of 22,000 civilians lost their lives.

At sea the Japanese navy fought the US navy in the two-day Battle of the Philippine Sea in June and Leyte Gulf in October 1944. In February 1945 US forces moved closer to Japan as they captured Iwo Jima, followed in April by Okinawa just to the south of the Japanese homeland. Japanese losses on Iwo Jima were 18,000 out of the total garrison of 20,000 and only 216 prisoners were taken. On Okinawa the 107,500-strong Japanese defence force died almost to a man along with a staggering 75,000 civilians. US losses of 7,000 soldiers and Marines on Okinawa were unacceptable and they forced the high command to consider what losses would be sustained if the Japanese homeland was invaded.

A crew of a Japanese Model 14 105mm anti-aircraft gun are given training in its maintenance on the Northern Pacific island of Kiska in the Aleutian group. The Model 14, introduced in 1925, was not a great gun and took a full 30 to 45 minutes to prepare for action. Kiska and the other Aleutian island of Attu were occupied by the Japanese on 6 and 7 June 1942. This was part of the Japanese plan to threaten the western coast of Alaska, but these men were soon isolated after their navy's defeat at the Battle of Midway. Kiska's 8,000-strong garrison was evacuated in July 1943 before the US navy landed there as it was for too isolated to hold any longer. The only living things found on the island were four dogs left behind by the Japanese when they were evacuated.

The commanding officer of the 2,600-strong garrison of the Aleutian island of Attu poses with his staff in 1942. On 30 May 1943 US Marines landed on the island and were resisted to the last man by the Imperial troops. Only twenty-eight of the garrison survived the battle for the island and most died in a suicidal banzai attack on the American landing force. As soon as the Japanese lost ground in the naval war in the Pacific in 1942–3 any hope of advancing from the Aleutians to other Northern Pacific islands was lost.

BRICKLEY
S-45

JAPANESE ALEUTIAN COMMANDER AND STAFF

(**Above**) Japanese soldiers manhandle a large anti-aircraft gun across an unidentified Pacific island as they prepare its defences. The gun appears to be a Model 3 120mm naval gun introduced into Japanese service in 1914. These guns were encountered on several islands during the US advance through the Pacific. Although it could be used as an anti-aircraft gun, it was intended to target Allied shipping as it approached the island. Guns like this were usually dug into bunkers and other strongpoints by Japanese engineers who became expert in building island defences.

(**Opposite, above**) Mortar crewmen of the Japanese army in the Pacific take part in training with their 81mm Type 97 mortar. The Type 97, introduced in 1937, was similar to most other 81mm mortars used by all other combatants. They were all based on the French Brandt mortar, which was universally copied by most of the world's armies. Ammunition for the Type 97 was of course interchangeable with the shells for the almost identical US mortar.

(**Opposite, below**) The crew of a medium mortar prepare to fire their 81mm mortar during a training exercise on an unidentified Pacific island with a case of shells at the ready. The crew have placed a Japanese flag on the ground in an attempt to protect them from possible friendly fire. Mortars were one of the most useful weapons in jungle warfare and the ease with which they could be moved was especially important. During the war the Japanese used three models of 50mm mortar, one 70mm, three types of 81mm, two models of 90mm and one 150mm mortar.

In this typical photograph from a propaganda magazine a Japanese soldier is greeted by happy Indonesian children. Japanese propaganda liked to portray the people of the former Dutch and British colonies in Malaya, Burma and the Dutch East Indies in this way. Although some people saw the Japanese as liberators from colonial oppression, the Japanese were usually to prove heavy handed and brutal in their treatment of the populations of occupied countries.

(**Opposite, above**) This poor quality photograph from 1942 shows a large parade that took place in Manila in the first months of the Japanese occupation. The Philippines was garrisoned by the 14th Area Army, which was expanded during the Japanese occupation to reach a total of 250,000 in October 1944. Japan's defence plans for the Philippines, known as *Sho-1*, would not actually be triggered until the US forces actually landed on the main island of Luzon. In the meantime, the Japanese were building defences in the interior of Luzon to wear down the American invaders.

(**Opposite, below**) The Japanese did not make use of snipers until they experienced the Chinese Nationalist snipers between 1937 and 1941 who had been trained by the German military mission. When they decided to train their own snipers the Japanese usually had one marksmen per platoon. These were not, however, the highly trained specialists used by other armies. During their advance through South-East Asia in 1941–2 the Imperial Army sometimes used snipers disguised as local civilians. These snipers were to go behind enemy lines and target enemy officers before melting back into the background. Although not great marksmen, the Japanese were adept at camouflaging themselves and were equipped to climb trees to wait for targets.

(**Opposite, above**) A three-gun battery of Type 88 75mm anti-aircraft guns take part in an alert on a South Pacific Island in 1944. The Type 88 was one of the main models of Japanese anti-aircraft guns in service at the start of the war, having entered service in 1928. As the US air force bombing of Japan began in earnest most of the Type 88s on the Pacific islands would if possible have been shipped back for homeland defence.

(**Opposite, below**) An NCO looks out nervously from the beach of a Pacific island for signs of Allied ships that could be bringing an invasion force in 1944. He is looking through an artillery battery commander's telescope and has his Model 38 1905 carbine at the ready. Many Pacific islands were virtually cut off from Japanese supplies and reinforcements as their ships were increasingly sunk by US ships, submarines and attack planes. When food ran out and with no way of reaching other islands many soldiers died of starvation in the last months of the war.

(**Above**) These despondent members of a captured Japanese work battalion are pictured after spending a few months in a US Marines' POW camp on Guadacanal in October 1942. These men were mostly naval reservists who had been passed as unfit for first-line service and were formed into construction crews. They were sent to Guadacanal to build an airfield and roads and were left behind by the Japanese when the US Marines took the island on 7 August. In the eyes of the Japanese these men were not worth saving and were sacrificed so that better troops could be evacuated.

(**Above**) These Special Naval Landing Force soldiers are posing on a beach on the Pacific island of Nauru in 1942. The garrison of this mineral rich island was made up of a 1,367-strong guard unit, 769 men of the Special Naval Landing Forces and a construction unit of 2,120 Korean workers. During its occupation the people of Nauru suffered terribly and a number of executions were carried out as well as most of the male population being removed to work as slave labourers. The island was one of many Japanese-occupied territories that were bypassed by the US armed forces as they advanced through the Pacific in 1944–5. It was estimated that Japanese Pacific garrisons totalling 101,762 soldiers and sailors were bypassed by the Allies.

(**Opposite, above**) Imperial Naval Landing Troops crouch with bayonets at the ready in the jungles of New Guinea where some of the most fierce fighting of the early Pacific War was fought. With New Guinea divided between Japanese and Australian held areas both sides were intent on gaining control of the whole vast island in 1942. Japanese offensives towards Port Moresby, the New Guinea capital, were launched in late August 1942. The Australians, fighting them with everything they had, finally threw them back in November when they were 35 miles from their target.

(**Opposite, below**) Heavily camouflaged Japanese troops receive instructions from their officer before going out on patrol in the New Guinea jungle. The Japanese were well trained in the use of camouflage and concealment and had prepared defensive positions in the jungles and swamps of the island. When the Australian forces moved on to the offensive in New Guinea in 1943 they were faced by a resolute enemy who fought them every step of the way. The officer in the photograph has his sword attached to his back so that he can draw it easily in the thick jungle.

(**Above**) This photograph sums up the kind of conditions faced by both the Japanese and their Australian foes along the Kokoda Trail in New Guinea in 1942–3. As they struggle through the undergrowth the soldiers are not helped by the ungainly nature of the Arisaka rifle. Both sides in the Pacific War eventually began to issue their troops with shorter rifles and carbines more suitable for the dense jungle conditions they faced. With no hope of re-supply these soldiers are carrying as much equipment and supplies as they can in their packs.

(**Opposite, above**) The crews of two Type 1 12.7mm heavy machine guns practise anti-aircraft firing from their beach-side bunkers on an unknown Pacific island in 1944. Type 1s were basically copies of the US Browning M1921 heavy machine gun and were used mainly as aircraft armament. Some were also converted, like these, with sights and flash hiders to be used as part of island anti-aircraft defences. Japan also made copies of the Lewis light machine gun, known as the 7.7mm M92, which were also used in the anti-aircraft role.

(**Opposite, below**) Prime Minister Hideki Tojo arrives at Kuching airfield on the Japanese-occupied island of Sarawak on 7 July 1943. Tojo was on a tour of Japanese-occupied territories and made a flying visit to the formerly British territory in the north of the island of Borneo. For any Imperial Army officer travelling from one area of the Pacific to another air travel was increasingly dangerous by this date. Garrisons of territories like Sarawak could expect little support from Japan and Tojo brought archery sets for the Japanese personnel as gifts.

Naval Landing Force machine-gunners are given training in preparation for their defence of a Pacific island in 1944. They are armed with a Type 99 light machine gun which was introduced into service in 1939 and was a larger calibre version of the earlier Type 96. The soldier seen here may well belong to one of the Special Naval Landing Forces organized for the defence of a particular island. Because the Imperial Navy was given command of most of the Pacific islands their personnel were expected to defend them against Allied offensives. The training given to Naval Landing Force troops was often regarded as inferior to that given to their army counterparts. This did not stop many of the Landing Troops garrisons of the various Pacific islands from fighting to the death in 1944–5.

(**Opposite, above**) A 13mm Model 93 anti-aircraft machine-gun crew practise its drill in a bunker on an unnamed Pacific island in 1944. The Model 93, introduced in 1933, was often mounted, as in this case, on a dual mount with a loader to feed the gun with thirty-round magazines. These crewmen are all Naval Landing Troops, who made up the majority of garrisons of the Pacific islands. All the men are wearing typical tropical uniforms with light cotton shirts, trousers and puttees and their helmets have canvas covers with the anchor insignia of the Naval Landing Force on the front.

(**Opposite, below**) Four members of a special assault unit are pictured before their mission to attack a US-held airfield in the Philippines in October 1944. They belong to the 1st Takasago Raiding Company, one of two units raised from the aboriginal hill tribesmen of the island of Formosa. Even though the Japanese were loath to recruit foreign troops into their army, they admired the fighting reputation of the Takasago volunteers. Carrying their traditional fighting knives and satchels full of explosives, these men were to be crash-landed on the island where the airfield was situated. Although the mission went badly and most of the raiders were killed, they did manage to destroy several US aircraft. It was reported that any survivors took the opportunity to escape Japanese service and withdrew into the jungle.

A dead soldier is seen in his dug-out on the island of Kwajalein, having shot himself rather than surrender to the victorious US Marines in February 1944. The island, which was part of the Marshall Island Group, was taken with relatively few US casualties between 31 January and 2 February. The Marshall Islands were made up of twenty-nine atolls and the defenders did not know where the US forces would strike. This meant that when the Marines landed on Kwajalein its garrison had been dispersed amongst other islands.

Chapter Ten

Japan's Defeat
(1944–5)

As the war in the Pacific turned disastrously against the Japanese in 1944–5 it was only a matter of time before Japan itself was threatened. Every Pacific island that was taken by the US army and Marines made it easier for their air force to bomb Japan. Huge air raids involving thousands of bombers were devastating Japanese cities and civilian casualties reached many thousands. In May 1945 US air raids on Tokyo destroyed 90,000 houses and hundreds of factories, further crippling the already outmatched Japanese military industries. From the outbreak of the war with the USA the Japanese had never competed with their enemy's war production. Between 1941 and 1945 the Japanese could only produce 28,963 artillery pieces – 22,780 light guns, 6,030 medium guns and 153 heavy guns. Even at its peak the Japanese war production never reached more than 10 per cent of the production of the USA. It was in the munitions works of the USA and Japan that the war was decided no matter how long the fighting continued.

While the US armed forces were advancing through the Pacific islands the battle for the Philippines was beginning. The forces available for the defence of the Philippines in 1944 were estimated at 275,000 and these were reinforced by divisions sent from China and Manchukuo. General Yamashita, the Japanese commander of the 14th Imperial Army on the Philippines, realized that his forces could not hope to defend all the Philippines islands. He decided to concentrate most of his resources on the main island of Luzon and the capital Manila. His forces were organized into the 'Shimbu', 'Kembu' and 'Shohu' Infantry Groups and the 2nd Tank Division, which had 300 tanks. The rest of the islands were defended by the 33rd Imperial Army, which had four infantry divisions and several mixed brigades. In some of the most brutal fighting of the Pacific War the liberation of the Philippines was to take from October 1944 until July 1945. It was to cost the Japanese a total of 320,000 casualties and 9,000 precious aircraft as well as hundreds of thousands of Filipino civilians. As the last fighting ended in the Philippines the Japanese were about to face up to the possibility of an invasion of their country.

By late 1944 and into early 1945 the Japanese army was still impressive on paper, but the quality of its troops had been diluted by conscripting youths, old men and the totally unfit. One of the royal princes inspected anti-aircraft units in Japan in autumn 1944 and was distressed to see one-eyed and crippled men manning the guns. This was a result of orders that military doctors were to pass 99 per cent of new recruits as fit no matter how unfit they actually were. In reality some men were simply not capable of serving in the army and in 1944 out of 1,468,000 checked only 1,000,000 were recruited. Japan had already dropped their rules about recruiting non-Japanese subjects of their empire and as a result thousands of Formosans and Koreans joined the army. At the same time the Japanese were trying to recruit auxiliaries in Malaya, Burma, Indonesia and the Philippines to help defend against Allied invasions.

By August 1945 the total manpower available for the defence of Japan was quoted as 2,350,000 front-line troops. These were organized into fifty-three infantry divisions, two tank divisions and brigades and four anti-aircraft defence divisions. In addition, there were reserve forces made up of 2,250,000 army workers and 1,300,000 navy workers and a Special Garrison Force of 250,000 men. On paper there was also 28 million men and women who were available for a national volunteer militia force if Japan was invaded. Shortages of weaponry and equipment were adversely affecting the Japanese Imperial Army by 1944–5 and there was no leather for webbing and a lack of ammunition. Rifles that were being produced in Japanese factories were often made of inferior materials and many were dangerous to use. Typical 'last-ditch' weapons were being made of whatever resources were available in a desperate attempt to arm the Japanese army. The only weapon that was easily produced in large numbers was the bamboo spear with which the Japanese intended to arm millions of soldiers and civilian volunteers if the Allies invaded.

One Japanese general summed up much of the thinking about the last-ditch resistance expected to be mounted by the populace. He said, 'If we could have 3 million bamboo spears we would be able to conquer Russia easily'. Another officer told a captive US officer:

> You have no chance of beating Japan. It took 20,000 American troops to defeat 2,000 Japanese soldiers on Attu Island. There are 100 million people in the Japanese Empire. It will take ten times 100 million to defeat Japan. To move such a force against Japan even if you had that many warriors, would be impossible. It will therefore become a matter of generations.

This fanatical attitude would, as the Allied Powers knew, result in suicidal resistance by the Japanese if an invasion of the country took place. Any invasion of Japan would result in hundreds of thousands of Allied soldiers' deaths as well as the loss of millions of Imperial troops and civilians.

As the USA decided whether to launch 'Operation Olympic' in 1946, two hammer blows finally ended Japanese resistance. First came the dropping of two atomic bombs by the USA on the Japanese cities of Hiroshima (6 August) and Nagasaki (9 August) causing an unprecedented level of destruction and loss of life. Secondly, the Soviet Red Army, with 1,500,000 men, invaded Manchuria on 8 August and quickly destroyed the 1,000,000-strong Kwangtung Army. It shows how deluded the Japanese leadership was that even after suffering such losses they still continued to think of continued resistance. Thankfully for the Japanese people and its army, common sense won out and Emperor Hirohito announced his country's surrender on 14 August. During the 1941–5 war the Japanese had lost 1,219,000 and its army, which began the war with such confidence, had been destroyed as a fighting force for ever.

Seen on manoeuvres in Japan in 1942, this Type 97 medium tank was the successor to the long-obsolete Type 89. With its distinctive radio antenna, which ran around the turret, it proved to be an advanced design for the period. Its main problem was the relatively ineffective main 57mm armament which was a low-velocity gun. At the outbreak of the Sino-Japanese War production of the Type 97 was accelerated and about 2,000 were made by Mitsubishi in total.

A ski trooper of the Imperial Army is seen during training in the mountains of Japan in 1943 before being sent to the China Theatre. Even as Japan's war situation worsened after 1942 their determination to retain their control of China meant that some reinforcements were sent there. This soldier is wearing typical winter uniform with a fur-lined hat and a double-breasted greatcoat with hood. Ski troops would, as in other armies, have been recruited when possible from snowy regions where the population already used skis.

This Formosan volunteer running at the double during training is one of 6,000 men from the island, occupied by Japan since 1895, who joined the Imperial Army between 1942 and 1944. Out of this total nearly 2,000 were from the aboriginal population of Formosa who were well regarded by the Japanese military. Starting in September 1944, as a result of a shortage of manpower 207,000 unwilling Formosans were conscripted and 30,304 died during the war.

Formosan aboriginal volunteers line up on parade in the last year of the war wearing their traditional *Takasagoan* fighting swords at their sides. They have been issued with tropical uniforms and have some kind of special insignia on the sides of their field caps. Having been subjects of the Chinese empire, they swapped colonial masters when the Japanese took control of Formosa in 1895. These aboriginal tribesmen had suffered abuse under both the Chinese and Japanese and had rebelled on several occasions. Having earned a reputation for toughness, they were earmarked by the Japanese as volunteers when manpower shortages began to affect Imperial Army numbers.

Three Korean POW guards pose for a studio photograph wearing their newly issued uniforms. As non-Japanese subjects of the empire, the camp guards were regarded as *Gunzoku*, or civilian volunteers of the Imperial Army. Their rank system as *Gunzoku* was made up of a white circle with a different coloured interlocking five-pointed star in the centre on their shoulders. Koreans had a reputation for brutality amongst the Allied POWs but were in turn treated badly by their Japanese masters.

(**Opposite, above**) Army paratroopers sit in the back of a plane taking them on a mission during the Pacific War. Although the original news caption says that this photograph was taken in 1944, it was probably from 1942. The Japanese formed two Parachute Raiding Regiments (1st and 2nd), made up of 425 men each, in time to take part in the 1941–2 offensive. In February 1942 the 2nd Regiment was employed in the taking of Palemburg in the Dutch East Indies. After losing all of their equipment at sea the 1st Regiment could not participate in the operation as planned and ended up fighting as infantry in Burma. In July 1943 a 5,575-strong divisional raiding unit was formed with gliders and support units but this was employed mainly as 'elite' infantry before the end of the war.

(**Opposite, below**) A unit of *Giretsu* Assault Commandos shakes hands with Captain Okuyama, the pilot who is to fly them on their suicide mission in 1945. The *Giretsu* units were formed from volunteers in the ranks of the Paratroopers who were crash-landed in bombers at various targets. Beginning in December 1944 with a 750-strong unit, a number of *Giretsu* missions were flown with the main targets being US airfields. 'Armed to the teeth' and carrying explosives, their intention was to cause as much damage as possible before fighting to the death. Larger operations involving several thousand commandos were planned for August 1945 but the end of the war stopped these.

(**Above, left**) A Japanese army NCO instructs women volunteers in the use of the bamboo spear in 1944. If the Allies had invaded Japan, these poorly armed 'amazons' would have been sent in waves against the troops. The officer is probably just returning to service from injury or has been seconded from one of the home-defence divisions to perform training. He wields a spear to instruct the women and is also armed with a 1935 pattern *shin-ginto* NCO's sword.

(**Above, right**) The cover of a Japanese propaganda magazine from 1945 shows a parade of boy volunteers for the defence of their homeland. By late 1944 any adult man could be called up for army service and doctors were told to pass 99 per cent of men as fit regardless of their condition. This led to young boys and disabled adults manning anti-aircraft guns and guarding factories and installations. Only 1 in 10 of volunteers usually had a rifle as these were given to the more experienced which left boys like this with bamboo spears. Arisaka Type 38 and 99 rifles that were actually issued in 1944–5 were often made from low-grade steel and were not heat treated making them dangerous to fire.

(**Opposite page**) Boy soldier volunteers are seen on parade in the closing months of the Second World War. These young boys and their female counterparts were meant to fight any Allied invasion of Japan with spears, knives and booby traps. Thankfully, 'Operation Olympic', the planned Allied invasion of the Japanese mainland, did not happen and most of these boys would live to see peace. We can only speculate how many millions of volunteers would have been sacrificed if it had gone ahead in 1946 as planned.

(**Above**) Japanese tankers of the Kwangtung Army in Manchuria take part in a night exercise during the winter of 1944–5. Although the Kwangtung Army had been stripped of much of its heavy equipment in the early 1940s, it still had 1,155 tanks. However, many of these were light tanks that were obsolete and would soon be crushed by the over 5,000 Russian tanks of the Soviet Far Eastern Army. These tanks are 15-ton Chi-Hai Medium tanks with a 57mm main armament, which although outclassed by Soviet tanks, were the best available.

(**Opposite, above**) The crews of an armoured unit of the Kwangtung Army gather in front of their tanks and motor vehicles during an exercise on the Mongolian steppe in the early 1940s. They have two different models of medium tank with a Type 89 in the foreground and a Type 97 in the distance. Also in the photograph are three six-wheeled command cars with special deep treaded tyres fitted for the rough terrain. All the tank crewmen have the cork crash helmet with armoured crew goggles and they are wearing summer overalls. It was units like this that faced the overwhelming onslaught of the Soviet Red Army when they invaded Manchuria in 1945.

(**Opposite, below**) This mechanized artillery unit with tracked artillery tractors would have been a rare sight by 1944. The tractors are Type 98 6-ton prime movers based on the chassis of the Type 97 tank and produced from 1938. Japanese industry could not hope to produce enough of these vehicles as the priority would have been given to tanks after 1941. They were used to pull 105mm and 150mm guns, although it was originally intended that they could also fulfil a reconnaissance role. Equipment like this was increasingly shipped to the Pacific Theatre after 1941, although some was retained with the Kwangtung Army in Manchukuo.

(**Opposite, above**) Massed ranks of Japanese Imperial Army tanks wait near Tokyo to hand over their vehicles to the Allies in August 1945. The tanks are Type 97 'Specials', an improved version of the original tank which was introduced into service in the late 1930s. This special version had a few more millimetres of armour plating and an adapted 47mm anti-tank gun in the turret. It had been developed as a result of the hard lessons learnt by the Japanese in their 1938–9 wars against the Soviet Union. Although it was not a match for most Allied tanks when it was introduced in 1942, the Type 97 Special was the best the Japanese had in any quantity.

(**Above**) A line-up of Type 3 medium tanks waiting to be inspected by Allied officers after the surrender of the Japanese Imperial Army in August 1945. This well-armed but poorly armoured tank was first made in 1943 in an attempt to combat the US Sherman tank. It had a 75mm gun and could at least match most Shermans in armament but had a total production of sixty. A Type 5 tank was developed which had the same main gun as the Type 3 with an additional 37mm gun in the front of the hull, but only a prototype was ever made.

(**Opposite, below**) Infantry of the Kwangtung Army line up in August 1945 to surrender their rifles and machine guns to a Soviet officer. Having been heavily defeated by the Soviets in their offensive to take Manchuria, these soldiers are happy to hand in their weapons. Over 1,000,000 men of the Kwangtung Army and their Manchukuoan puppet allies surrendered to the Red Army. Many of these weapons were to end up in the hands of Chinese Communist troops during the coming Civil War.

Demoralized Japanese troops in Hong Kong sit around waiting to be processed by the Allied authorities after their surrender in August 1945. In the aftermath of the liberation of Hong Kong a number of Japanese officers and military police were killed by the people they had abused during the occupation. The surrender of the British territory was complicated by the insistence of Chiang Kai-shek, the Chinese leader, that Hong Kong should be surrendered to him. A compromise meant that the territory was surrendered to the Chinese who then handed it back to the British, the official ceremony taking place on 16 September.

Smartly turned out Japanese soldiers hold their Type 98 rifles up for inspection by US troops as they surrender in Korea in September 1945. The total number of Imperial troops in Korea at the end of the war was 260,000, with those in the North under the official command of the Kwangtung Army. Those in the South were under the command of the 17th Area Army with three infantry divisions. These men were fortunate to be in one of the few regions of the Japanese empire that saw little or no fighting in the war.

US soldiers search newly captured Japanese soldiers in Manila in the Philippines. The prisoners have been given uniforms to wear, including shorts featuring the letters 'PW' to identify them as prisoners of war. The Japanese who chose to surrender would not want to be mistaken for their Filipino allies, the Makapili. These traitors were usually killed instantly by the civilian population who had suffered at their hands during the Japanese occupation. Some Japanese units continued to resist the US forces until 15 August on the Philippines island of Mindanao.